DAD THE FAMILY
MENTOR

DAD THE FAMILY
MENTOR

◆

DAVE SIMMONS

VICTOR BOOKS
A DIVISION OF SCRIPTURE PRESS PUBLICATIONS INC.
USA CANADA ENGLAND

SERIES

Dad, the Family Shepherd
P.O. Box 21445
Little Rock, AR 72221
(501) 221-1102

Unless otherwise noted, Scripture references are from the *New American Standard Bible*, © the Lockman Foundation 1960, 1962, 1963, 1968, 1971, 1972, 1973, 1975, 1977. Used by permission. Other references are from the *Holy Bible, New International al Version* ® (NIV). Copyright © 1973, 1978, 1984, International Bible Society. Used by permission of Zondervan Publishing House.

Copyediting: Jerry Yamamoto and Barbara Williams
Cover Design: Joe DeLeon

Library of Congress Cataloging-in-Publication Data

Simmons, Dave.
    Dad the family mentor / by Dave Simmons.
        p.   cm.   —   (Dad the family shepherd series ; v. 3)
    Includes bibliographical references.
    ISBN: 0-89693-948-0
    1. Fathers — Religious life. 2. Fathers — Conduct of life.
    I. Title. II. Series: Simmons, Dave. Dad the family shepherd
    series ; v. 3.
    BV4843.S575   1992
    248.8'421 — dc20   92-16572
                                                                   CIP

Contents

DAD THE FAMILY SHEPHERD SERIES

WISDOM				PRACTICAL TECHNIQUES			
PHILOSOPHY				FUNCTIONS			
WHAT YOU MUST KNOW		WHAT YOU MUST BE		WHAT YOU MUST DO			
SIGNIFICANCE		SCOPE		SURVEY OF FUNCTIONS			
1	2	3	4	5	6	7	8
VOLUME 1 — DAD the FAMILY COACH							

COACHING TIPS							
LOVE		BOND		LEAD			
1	2	3	4	5	6	7	8
VOLUME 2 — DAD the FAMILY COUNSELOR							

EQUIP							
TEACH		TRAIN		TRACK		TEND	
1	2	3	4	5	6	7	8
VOLUME 3 — DAD the FAMILY MENTOR							

Dedication

To my children:

Helen Dawn Simmons
The joy and light — light of my life

Brandon Paul Simmons
Whom I respect as much as any man I know

Acknowledgment

Even though my name appears on the cover of the Dad the Family Shepherd Series as author, I would like to acknowledge my wife, Sandy Simmons, as the true heart and soul of these books. The Lord orchestrated Sandy like a golden harp where the chords of her heart respond to the needs of children.

Sandy is my major source of inspiration, aspiration, and information on the nature and care of children. My role has been to bring to you the vision of child-raising as seen through masculine eyes of fatherhood, but I could not have done this project without Sandy's wisdom and encouragement.

Coaching Tips:
How to get the most from this book

Coaching Tip One: START AN E-TEAM.
Real Men Need Real Men

Dad, the Family Shepherd
E-TEAM

Iron sharpens iron, so one man sharpens another.

— Proverbs 27:17

For best results, this course on fatherhood should be:

1. Ingested internally at the rate of one chapter per week.
2. Digested in the company of a few trusted men, an E-Team.
3. Invested in the lives of your family slowly but surely.

This calls for an E-Team (Encouragement Team), a small group of five to seven men who meet weekly to study family-life principles and to motivate each other to apply what they learn. An E-Team functions as a vehicle to get you from the valley of intention to the plateau of success. An E-Team converts ambition to action. It transfers desire for better fatherhood to changed behavior patterns in the home.

An E-Team is the only way I know to guarantee steady progress. There are no shortcuts. Progress requires men committed to help each other work hard at fatherhood over a long period of time.

Take the initiative and recruit an E-Team to go through this course with you. Read the instructions on how to start your E-Team.

An E-Team gives a man:

Encouragement
Understanding
Inspiration
Solutions
Challenge
Accountability

E-TEAM INSTRUCTIONS

In order to establish an E-Team and successfully lead it through this course, follow these steps.

1. ACQUIRE THE E-TEAM CAPTAIN'S MANUAL IN VOLUME 1: *DAD THE FAMILY COACH* OR SEND TO Dad The Family Shepherd FOR IT.

2. RECRUIT YOUR TEAM.
   Challenge four to six other men to meet together with you for eight weeks to complete the course. Mention that each meeting has a reading assignment that must be completed beforehand and there will be a brief, practical, useful application project following each session. Make sure each man gets a copy of the book in time to prepare for the first meeting. Be sure they know the exact time, place, and assignment for the first meeting.

3. MAKE ASSIGNMENTS
   Instruct each man to read "The Scouting Report" and Chapter 1, "Dad the Family Sage" before the first meeting. Remind them to bring the book, notepaper, and pencil to the meeting. Call them a few days before the first meeting to remind them of everything.

4. FOLLOW THE E-TEAM GUIDE AT THE END OF EACH SESSION.
   At the meeting, just follow the E-Team Guide at the end of each session.

Coaching Tip Two: STUDY THE CONTEXT.

Turn to Appendix A and read the summary of Volume 1, *Dad the Family Coach* and a synopsis of the fatherhood function "To Equip."

Coaching Tip Three:
SCHEDULE A VIDEO CONFERENCE.

Dave Simmons' message on fatherhood is available on video. The video package contains the exact same eight hours of the Dad the Family Shepherd live conference that Dave has given throughout the nation since 1984.

The video package is designed to be used for conferences and is not for sale. It is the convenient alternative to a live conference and has been proven to be just as effective as the live conference. (For information on how to sponsor a video conference in your church, see Appendix B.)

Coaching Tip Four:
START A FATHERHOOD INSTITUTE.

Consider these questions. Does your church have:

A fatherhood basic training process?
A fatherhood wellness and enhancement process?
A fatherhood diagnostic and remedial training process?
A fatherhood crisis center and an intensive care unit?

The Fatherhood Institute is a comprehensive fatherhood training package specifically designed so a church can easily insert it intact and equip their men to become more effective family shepherds. It features a system of set courses based on a tri-semester format with courses offered in the fall, winter, and spring. (Contact Dad the Family Shepherd for more information on the Fatherhood Institute.)

Foreword

A Father—one of the easiest titles to get; one of the most difficult positions to fill.

Most of us men have no problem asking the investment advice of a financial planner and have no reason to hide from other men that we regularly seek help in this area of our life.

Most of us wouldn't hesitate to hire a golf pro to help us tame a slice and look for every opportunity to tell others, complete with a demonstration, of the secret pro-grip "guaranteed to keep your ball dry."

Yet few of us would ever ask the advice of others on how to be a better father. In the most important and perhaps most difficult area of our lives, we are afraid to ask for help, unable to admit our failures, and reluctant to share our fears with those who might help.

"Dad" is our most important title. It comes without business cards, but has plenty of perks and many challenges. The stakes are large. The church has our children for 1 percent of their week, school another 16 percent. The rest falls on us; the home environment we provide; the time we give.

Healthy families require a strong, competent president and chief executive officer—the father. All other family members take their cue from him. The family direction, the family culture, the family survival flows from the father. Yet, too often the father neglects his role as President of the Family to place all his time, energy, and creativity in his role as the third Minion in the fourth Cubicle of the XYZ Corporation. The choice is foolish. The results are disastrous.

As a result, the state of fatherhood in this country is in a depression that no tax cut, no change in economic policy can remedy. The typical father cannot relate to his wife, he is distant from his children, he is insecure about his role, and he is confused about what solutions he should pursue. Worst of all, even if he had the courage to break the invisible barrier of asking for advice, he wouldn't know where to go.

Fatherhood needs a booster shot and the Dad the Family Shepherd series of Encouragement (E-Team) courses are the prescription. Dave Simmons has established a practical, down-to-earth, realistic means to help. The approach begins with a group of fathers who want to help themselves and each other grow. The curriculum is fast-paced but not unrealistic, easy to follow but not easy to escape without immediate solutions to build a lifetime of good fathering.

Dad the Family Mentor, Volume 3 in the series, addresses the fourth of the Four Fatherhood Functions—to equip your children. In it, Dave Simmons presents a balanced child-raising process that supports discipline with a foundation of preliminary input, reasonable expectations, and practical coaching tips.

When men get together to encourage each other and find biblical solutions to their specific family problems, things begin to happen. Confidence is built, relevant answers are found, and friendships grow. It is a winning combination—a good game plan with sound biblical insight and relevant applications, and a team of committed fathers to run with.

The results of faithful fatherhood far outweigh any career climb, any economic windfall, or any position of power and fame that can be imagined. The game plan is ready, the team is in place, the time is now.

Howard G. Hendricks
Chairman, Center of Christian Leadership
Distinguished Professor, Dallas Theological Seminary

The Scouting Report

*"Those Individuals who do not
look upon themselves as a line
connecting the past with the
future do not perform their
duty to the world."*

—*Daniel Webster*[1]

Death is good at making us think about life. There is nothing like trudging past a forest of tombstones on the way to church that will rivet people to a sermon about eternal life. A stroll among the dead brings a somber stillness as we imagine their thoughts fluttering about like the soft rustle of crispy autumn leaves scuttling across a woods' path. A cemetery creates a solemn mood for profound reflections about our ancestors and their encounters with life. Yes, death makes us serious. It makes us think big thoughts about priorities, values, and significance. Death does wonders for profound contemplation on life.

TOMBSTONE FATHERHOOD

What epitaph would you like your children to write on your tombstone? This question was asked of more than 8,000 men who attended our Dad the Family Shepherd conference over a period of six years, and here is a sample of what they wrote. Unfortunately, many of us had a negative experience growing up with our fathers that has left a bitter memory in our hearts. Read the epitaphs these men wrote for their fathers and note the bitterness and disappointment.

Since these men have grown up under a particular fathering style that caused them a lot of pain, they strongly hope they do not subject their children to the same legacy. Fortunately, other men had great experiences with nurturing, effective fathers and want to leave a positive epitaph engraved on their tombstones.

As you reflect on these sobering thoughts from these men,

AN EPITAPH FOR OUR FATHERS	
Texas	Here Lies My Dad Always gone: still is
California	Here Lies My Dad He did not demonstrate love to his sons
Minnesota	Here Lies My Dad A hardworking man full of pride who died lonely
Illinois	Here Lies My Dad If your actions matched your talk, you would be awesome
Colorado	Here Lies My Dad He had time for the community but not enough for his kids

Figure 1

think about the time in the future when you will be buried. What would you like your children to cut into your granite gravestone? If you continue on your present level and style of fatherhood practice, will it lead to the epitaph you desire? With this in mind, do you think you may want to modify or adjust your fatherhood practices?

AN EPITAPH FOR OUR FATHERS	
Texas	Here Lies My Dad One of my best friends A real neat guy
California	Here Lies My Dad A man who encouraged his children to reach for their dreams
Colorado	Here Lies My Dad A man to model my own life by and try to equal
Florida	Here Lies My Dad One of the men I most admire

Figure 2

HERO FATHERHOOD

What if your whole generation had a single tombstone? What would be the epitaph written on it? It might not be very positive, and one of the major reasons lies with the current confusion on male roles, masculinity, and fatherhood. David Blankenhorn, president of the Institute for American Values, reports on the death of fatherhood and its meaning.

> Much of the national debate about family decline tacitly assumes that the dilemma centers on women's roles, choices and responsibilities. But this assumption overlooks the single most troubling family trend in our era: male flight from family life.
>
> Approximately one of every four children in the nation is growing up without a father in the home . . . The growth of fatherlessness constitutes a clear and present danger. What are the social consequences of a cultural ethos that refuses to celebrate the ideal of the man who puts his family first? Surely this missing language—this cultural black hole where the ideals of husband and father ought to be—helps explain today's shocking rise of fatherlessness.[2]

He goes on to lament the way our culture smirks at the phrase "a good family man" and seeks to replace it with new politically correct modern ideals that women find unquenching but men find silly. He suggests that we should appreciate the difference between "parent" and "father," "spouse" and "husband."

No wonder young men are confused about the fathering role. They face potent pressure to adopt the putrid male role models that our culture currently attempts to fob off on men: the wet/bright-eyed androgynous lush (Prince, Michael Jackson); the testosteronic teutonic titan (Rambo); the sociopath cowboy/detective (Dirty Harry); the inept, asinine, bewildered, sexually bland dupe (token white male in scads of sitcoms); the sex-obsessed bachelor (the bartender in "Cheers"); the horny student geek/nerd (the studs in myriads of beach and college movies); the blood-spraying, lurid Mafia good-fellows; the gonad-brained super jock; and the paranoid, conniving, vain, iron-hearted, profit-grubbing businessman.

What are the young men of America to think when Pee Wee Herman gets a standing ovation at the MTV awards for indecent exposure, when L.A. Laker James Worthy gets a standing ovation from the fans for getting arrested for soliciting a prostitute, when television focuses on every lurid sexually explicit detail concerning the William Kennedy Smith rape trial and the Supreme Court nomination hearings of Clarence Thomas?

Where is the sensible, balanced, appropriate, effective, faithful-to-his-family male model in our entertainment, business, political, and marketing world? In the inner city, the suburbs, and the countryside, young boys thirst for positive hero models. Roger Staubach is one man who stood up for the family in an incident as related by my pastor, Bill Parkinson.

> In an interview on national TV, sports announcer Phyllis George asked Roger Staubach, Dallas Cowboy quarterback, this question: "How do you feel when you compare yourself to Broadway Joe Namath who is so sexually active and has a different woman on his arm every time you see him?" Roger answered, "Phyllis, I'm sure I am as sexually active as Joe. The difference is all of mine is with the same woman." TOUCHDOWN![3]

The next generation of fathers needs exposure to this kind of heroism from you as well as from public figures. You may be the only hero some boy will ever see.

MISSING-LINK FATHERHOOD

Unfortunately, too many of today's children will not have hero fathers. What happened to our culture over the past several generations that caused such deterioration and degradation of the American male?

Why Johnny Can't Father

This is the generation of mislocated children. Parents have lost sight of kids. We have entered the age of phantom fathers and rent-a-womb mothers. Getting born and growing up has again become the high risk venture that it was several centuries ago.

From Power Father to Flower Child

Maybe the stock market crash, the Great Depression, the dust bowls of the Great Plains, and World War I sucked the juices of fatherhood out of our American fathers of the twenties. Their sons endured harsh Depression childhoods, left home, and plunged right into World War II. Maturing under non-nurturant survival-fathers and hardened by battle, they became the soldier-fathers of the forties and sired the famous crop of babies soon dubbed the Baby Boomers.

With visions of depression and battle dancing in his head, this "John Wayne" type, forties father sold his heart to plunder the riches of the postwar boom. He flourished, soon cruising the suburbs in a station wagon and grilling hamburgers on the patio. Presto! He had become Dad the Family Provider.

Unfortunately, he had also become Dad the Family Stranger. He withheld his macho self from his wife and children. She promptly stepped out of the kitchen into the work force, and the kids stepped out of the backyard into Woodstock.

The hypermasculine fathers of the forties and fifties raised paternally deprived children, who grew up and had to kick the bad habits of the world instead of the bad Hitlers of the world. Ironically, the power-fathers of the forties sired the flower-children of the sixties. The warrior-dad begat the peace-child. Their daughters burned their bras while their sons burned their draft cards.

From happy hippies came eager yuppies. The anti-establishment youth of the sixties went to Woodstock to make a major statement and left to become a major market. They became the double-career generation and brought new meaning to the term "neglectful parents."

Parenthood became a franchise industry. Child raising became a joint venture between parents and outside institutions—the bear-and-share theory. The schools took over value clarification and taught situational ethics. The media preempted amusement and desensitized and androgenized the children. The government shuffled them into numbers and dealt them into quotas. The legal and psychiatric literature rendered them guiltless and nonresponsible.

The Spawn-and-Pawn Theory

These institutionally raised and mutually fostered kids now come to parenthood in the eighties. They were excluded from the standard eighteen-year parenthood training and modeling course from their parents. Untutored and unmentored in parenting skills, they were reduced to the spawn-and-pawn theory of parenting—you spawn them and pawn them off on others.

Parents now function as brood stock. They pause in the mad flight for personal fulfillment to evacuate the womb and whoop on down the fast track of life. They deposit their bottle-fed babies in kiddie-care covens and school cells, keep them in Reeboks, straighten their teeth, and call it child raising.

Perhaps, as in Israel of old, the chain of fatherhood has been wrenched, if not broken. As fatherhood in America has diminished, the pain in the family has shot up. The following trends from the Center for Fatherhood Research (1988) indicate the seriousness of the problem:

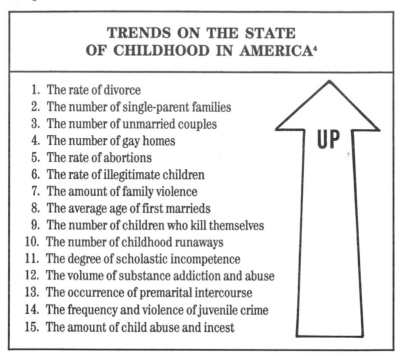

TRENDS ON THE STATE OF CHILDHOOD IN AMERICA[4]

1. The rate of divorce
2. The number of single-parent families
3. The number of unmarried couples
4. The number of gay homes
5. The rate of abortions
6. The rate of illegitimate children
7. The amount of family violence
8. The average age of first marrieds
9. The number of children who kill themselves
10. The number of childhood runaways
11. The degree of scholastic incompetence
12. The volume of substance addiction and abuse
13. The occurrence of premarital intercourse
14. The frequency and violence of juvenile crime
15. The amount of child abuse and incest

Figure 3

Another way to look at the state of childhood in America is to check what happens to our youth in an average day. See Figure 4.

With these prevailing winds blowing through our culture, how do you set your sail and plot your course? For your family to be one of the healthy ones, what do you need to know to do what you need to do to get what you want from your fatherhood practice? What are your specific goals? What changes in fatherlore and fathercraft need to be made? What guiding principles will ensure success? What are the major threats to your fathering practices?

"CRUISE MISSILE" FATHERHOOD

What you need to know to do about fatherhood breaks down into five major areas of concern. These areas must be addressed to begin

ONE DAY IN THE LIFE OF AMERICA'S CHILDREN[5]	
2,795	Teens get pregnant.
1,106	Teens have abortions.
372	Teens miscarry.
7,742	Teens become sexually active.
623	Teens get syphillis or gonorrhea.
1,849	Children are abused or neglected.
3,288	Children run away.
1,629	Children are put in adult jails.
135,000	Children bring a gun to school.
437	Children are arrested for drinking or DWI.
211	Children are arrested for drug abuse.
2,989	Children see their parents divorce.
1,512	Teens drop out of school.

Figure 4

the process of fatherhood enhancement. These areas are: Your mission, the environment, your identity, your skills, and each child. They are best seen in relationship by using the analogy of a cruise missile. See Figure 5.

Fatherhood Mission

A mission statement is a leadership tool that clearly identifies two things:

1. A picture of intended results at the end of the path.
2. A clarification of principles that designate the path.

A Fatherhood Mission Statement gives you a precise statement of what you want your fatherhood practice to accomplish and sets forth an unchanging standard, or constitution, that will best ensure the achievement of your mission. It will function as a document that keeps you on track by providing objective criteria for making judgments and decisions.

It helps you see fatherhood in its true perspective and gives you a benchmark for evaluation. The true measure of fatherhood is not what you accomplish with your children but the extent of godliness in your grandchildren. In Deuteronomy 4:9, Moses wrote:

THE FATHERHOOD CRUISE MISSILE

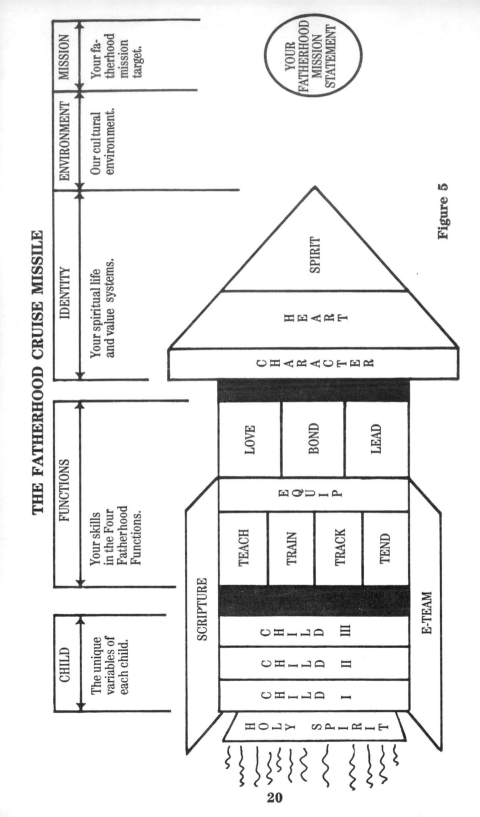

Figure 5

Only give heed to yourself and keep your soul diligently, lest you forget the things which your eyes have seen, and lest they depart from your heart all the days of your life; but make them known to your sons and your grandsons.

Without a mission statement on fatherhood, you become susceptible to the scripts that other people, organizations, and circumstances assign you. Fatherhood then gets misplaced, shunted aside, or neglected, and eventually the epitaph your children write for you might not turn out so well.

You need to write your own Fatherhood Mission Statement and let it serve as a guiding north star for your fatherhood practice.

Fatherhood Environment

The cultural environment of the fathers of the twenties and thirties was radically different from that of the fathers of today. Even though the fathering principles and the Four Fatherhood Functions (Love, Bond, Lead, and Equip) remain the same, the practice and technique of fatherhood must be altered to be relevant for today. Even if your forefathers fathered with excellence in their day and passed their expertise on to you, you will still struggle because you are in a different ballgame altogether.

My dad, Major Amos E. Simmons (U.S. Army), grew up in a clapboard shack on a dirt road deep in the pine forests of Southern Louisiana during the Great Depression in a family with nine children. Since my grandpa, Ole Man Luther, was a lumberjack and farmer, my dad spent many long days cutting timber, planting crops, weeding the garden, collecting eggs, and feeding livestock side by side with Grandpa. Dad hauled logs with oxen and plowed with mules. He didn't spend a lot of time in school. As a child, Dad had no radio, TV, tennis shoes, bike, records, room of his own, or car. As a boy, Dad never had a fast food meal, visited a barbershop, went to a shopping center, saw a movie, or looked at a porno magazine. He wore overalls every day of his childhood.

I didn't raise Helen and Brandon in a cultural environment like that. The world they grew up in is drastically different and bewildering in its complexity and destructive influence on children. Thus, my fathering style had to be dramatically different from that of Ole Man Luther.

Most parents fail to realize how much World War II, the boom of the fifties, and the rebellion of the sixties have altered the environment in which our families exist, adding extra stress on parenthood as a result. H. Stephen Glenn, in his excellent book, *Raising Self-Reliant Children in a Self-Indulgent World*, contrasts the norms of the thirties with the norms of the eighties.

MAJOR TRANSITIONS IN LIFESTYLE[6]		
Characteristics	Norm 1930	Norm 1980
Family interaction	high	low
Value system	homogeneous	heterogeneous
Role models	consonant	dissonant
Logical consequences	experienced	avoided
Intergenerational associations	many	few
Education	less	more
Level of information	low	high
Technology	low	high
Nonnegotiable tasks	many	few
Family work	much	little
Family size	large	small
Family dominant	extended	nuclear
Step/blended/single-parent families	10–15%	35–42%
Class size (K–12)	18–22	28–35
Neighborhood schools	dominant	rare

Figure 6

As a result of this cataclysmic shift in culture, Glenn sees this difference in the children of then and the children of now:

Their children usually continued working hard to improve the land or business their parents had worked and sometimes died for. In so doing, they continued to develop greater capabilities. Today, by comparison, our children seem astonishingly incapable. And yet they face an unprecedented wealth of possibilities. Our challenge today is to help our children develop the self-reliance, commitment, and skills that children learned as a matter of course thirty to fifty years ago. They

learned these skills because they had roles to play in the economic
lives of their families, and because they grew up in stable cultures in
which they followed well-established precedents.[7]

In those days, the culture was family friendly, and kids matured in
a healthy way by just developing through the natural child track.
Fatherhood drifted downstream. Today, fatherhood fights against the
current. Fatherhood must struggle to overcome the undertow of family
hostile elements in our cultural environment. Dads must go out of
their way to practice fathercraft. Therefore, Dads need to digest new
ideas on fatherhood techniques, like the books in this series, and get
constant creative input on application from an E-Team.

Fatherhood Identity

Children do who you are, not what you say. Who you are counts
more than what you say when it comes to child raising. Children
can recover from a thousand mistakes as long as the heart is right.
Therefore, be true to thine own heart, and thy fatherhood craft shall
be stout!

Christian character comes from a heart in harmony with God.
When a man trusts Jesus Christ as his Savior, the Holy Spirit enters
his heart and gives him a personal relationship with God. A consistent walk with God results in the kind of heart that builds godly
character.

Fatherhood is a function of quality character, not of slick personality. Excellent fathers work from a foundation of proven ethical
principles, convictions, and good character, out of which flows
effective fathering practices, techniques, and skills.

Strong fathers eschew the superficial personality ethic that uses
fathering skills as manipulative gimmicks. The quick-fix, positive
mental imaging, boy-am-I-enthusiastic approach does not a high
caliber father make. Men who try to get by on mere personality
make flimsy fathers.

There is no one biblically approved personality or fathering style,
only biblically approved character. There is plenty of room and
flexibility for a variety of fathering personalities, and all can be
successful. Think, for instance, of the vast variety of coaching
styles of the coaches who won the past five Super Bowl games.

Whatever your fathering personality, you can be a winning coach
as long as you abide by these four nonnegotiables:

1. The integrity and spiritual maturity of your heart.
2. Your love and creative demonstration of affection for your wife in the presence of your children.
3. Your performance of the Four Fatherhood Functions.
4. Your mixture of high support and firm control (see chap. 7).

Wise fathers concentrate on developing godly character and let the skills flow from the inside out. King David had it right: "So he shepherded them according to the integrity of his heart, and guided them with his skillful hands" (Ps. 78:72).

Fatherhood Skills

All of the actions that a father ever has to perform can be sorted into four major classifications, which I call the Four Fatherhood Functions: To Love, Bond, Lead, and Equip. This series of three books covers these four functions in a structure shown on page 6. Volume 1, *Dad the Family Coach*, covers the heart and character of a father and an introduction to the Four Fatherhood Functions. Volume 2, *Dad the Family Counselor*, gives details on how to Love, Bond, and Lead. This volume, *Dad the Family Mentor*, covers how to Equip your children, which requires this four-step process:

THE EQUIPPING PROCESS

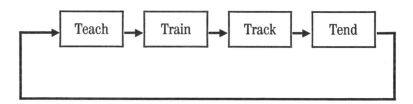

Figure 7

Strong fathers have mastered the Four Fatherhood Functions to the point that they have become habits; they perform them seemingly by instinct. But they didn't start out that way. They had bad fathering habits that needed to be broken, and they had new ones that needed to be formed. Developing a new habit is certainly difficult, and it requires the following four steps:

Desire + Insight + Skill + Practice = Habit

This book presents the insight and skills, but you must furnish the desire and commitment to practice. The greatest asset I know of to help ensure consistency in your desire and practice is an E-Team.

The Child

One of the reasons fatherhood taxes the brightest of us is the complexity of it. You must know what to do in a vast number of situations over a long period of time with each unique child.

The father must perform the Four Fatherhood Functions with each child through nine distinctive developmental phases. This makes thirty-six separate little windows ("fathering facets") you need to deal with. You must adjust the performance of each Fatherhood Function to the demands of each developmental stage.

The equation becomes even more complex when you consider the uniqueness of each child. Have you ever marveled at how different two or more children can be, though coming from the same parents and home? Children are like snowflakes: No two are alike. I had an eleven-year argument with Gracella, my sister, over which color is more beautiful, red or green. Margaret, another sister, loves cats. She's obsessed with them. She thinks they should be collected while I think they should be mounted. My little brother, Doug Simmons (6'6", 270 lbs.), is a big soft teddy bear. He attacks life with a pillow while I resemble the high-strung grizzly bear and smack life with a cudgel.

Your family also is a unique collection of individuals. To determine the full complexity of fatherhood in your family, multiply the Four Fatherhood Functions times the nine child development phases and you come up with the thirty-six separate fathering variables.

Now, multiply this total times the number of your children to find the total number of "fathering facets." If you have four children, you have 144 separate "fathering facets" to keep you on your toes.

That's why no book or conference will ever teach you everything you need to know about fatherhood. You need a heart of integrity, a smattering of fathering know-how, a capacity to solve problems, and the advice and counsel from men in your E-Team, who know you and your family members, to help you know what to do in the myriads of "fathering facets."

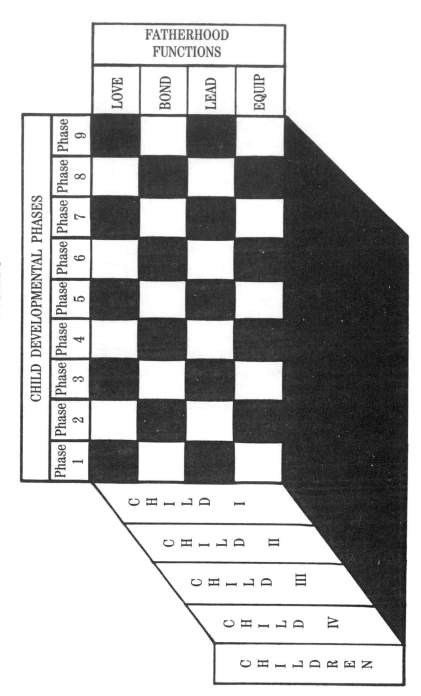

THE "FATHERHOOD FACETS"

Figure 8

SCIENTIFICALLY ANALYZED FATHERHOOD

Fathers can gain an incredible advantage when they know precisely what their fathering style is and how to relate it to the unique variables of each individual child. There are some excellent tools now available to help you discover the mystery of these invisible dynamics that ebb and flow within your family. Dad the Family Shepherd can provide you with two outstanding instruments that would be a great aid in your efforts to enhance your fathering skills. See Appendix D for more information.

RELATIONAL FATHERHOOD

I have often wondered why there are so few biblical passages on the specific topic of child raising. There are many that deal with fatherhood and tell fathers what principles of life to teach children, but the Bible doesn't tell us much about the best way to teach. It tells us a little, but not much, about child psychology and developmental stages. Where do we find biblical information on things like learning preferences, potty training, and birth order behavior?

Sandy, my wife, suggested (and I agree) that the Bible doesn't offer massive advice on parent/child relationships because the extensive biblical material pertaining to adult relationships applies to children as well. When the Bible tells us to love one another, bear one another's burdens, confess to one another, confront one another, encourage one another, respect and honor one another, and not to criticize, defame, defraud, cheat, or lie to one another, it means to relate to our children in this way as well. They are little people, and all the people relationship principles also apply to them.

"LISTICAL" FATHERHOOD

Beware of lists. Lists have been the downfall of many a good man. Watch out whenever an author or speaker starts getting mystical and listical; that is, he gives a list here and a list there, nine insights into this, five principles about that, six steps to something with a formula for it.

Watch out for me. I too am a mystical, listical teacher.

You need to keep in mind that the issues of fathering are incredibly complex, and each father deals with countless variables. No list will apply to all situations. Lists can build a false sense of security because they make a man feel as though he has a prescription that will fix things right up. I do not promote formula fatherhood.

27

So, why do I list my lists? Because I want to have you think seriously through the process as intelligently and logically as possible at least once. If you just follow along and understand the connections between the steps and how the whole process generally flows, you will be much better off than if you never think through these things at all.

The perfect scenario is to read a chapter, take note of the important stuff, DISCUSS IT AT GREAT LENGTH WITH THE MEN IN YOUR E-TEAM, and then just let it fill your tank. When you need it, you will discover a way to get it out and use it. Just let it become a part of you. Your brain will figure where to put it, and your child will force it out of you when the need arises.

MENTOR FATHERHOOD

A father is a mentor. In addition to performing the first three Fatherhood Functions—Love, Bond, and Lead—he also shoulders the responsibility of a mentor—to Equip his children with the competence to cope with life and get things done, to achieve, to be proactive and accomplish goals and projects. A mentor makes his protégés successful. He does whatever it takes to transfer whatever it takes to help his followers equal or surpass himself. Ted Engstrom, in his book *The Fine Art of Mentoring*, writes:

> A mentor provides modeling, close supervision on special projects, individualized help in many areas — discipline, encouragement, correction, confrontation, and a calling to accountability. Mentoring is a term describing the process of developing a man or a woman to his or her maximum potential in Jesus Christ in every vocation.[8]

This book is dedicated to help you master the skills of mentoring your children. Again, I ask, "What epitaph would you like your children to write on your tombstone?" I challenge you to E-Team this book and begin mentoring your children with much vigor and great style.

The Fatherhood Function: To Teach

Chapter One
Dad the Family Sage

TEACH		TRAIN		TRACK		TEND	
1	2	1	2	1	2	1	2

"Until I can risk appearing imperfect in your eyes,
without fear that it will cost me something,
I can't really learn from you."
— *Rudolph Dreikurs*[1]

MAGIC IN A FANTASY WORLD

He established himself as one of the greatest athletes and role models in the history of the world. He fought his way out of the ghetto to achieve spectacular success. His basketball talent, his brilliant smile, his alluring personality, his team-centered leadership, his upbeat attitude, and his generosity made him one of the most beloved public figures in the world. He conquered life. His obstacles lay strewn at his feet.

The "King of Basketball" made it big. But he lost it all. Earvin "Magic" Johnson excelled above them all in the land of the living, but he crossed over to the land of the dying. In an emotional scene on national TV, Magic shocked the world with the revelation of his licentious lifestyle and his acquisition of the cursed HIV virus.

Mr. Personality lived in Magic Johnson instead of Mr. Character. Everybody loved Magic the Image, but we didn't know about Magic the User—a man who used numerous women as objects of selfish sexual gratification, knowing full well about the high possibility of his contracting and disseminating the AIDS horror. He had the skills, but he didn't have the heart to finish the game. Because he didn't abide by the timeless ethical principles that govern human behavior, he lost his basketball career—and he may lose his life.

My friend and pastor, Robert Lewis, wrote Magic a letter that says it perfectly·

> From a hero I expected more. I wanted to hear Earvin share his heart, not "Magic" play the crowd. I wanted tears, not that big smile; for you to say you were deceived, that life is more than a game. I wanted to hear you tell young people, my kids especially, that you regret the hundreds of women you used as playthings and sex objects and who in turn used you! But, instead, my boys heard you say that it's okay to use women, just be safe. For my daughters, I wanted you to apologize to the women you no doubt gave the AIDS virus to. They are going to die, Earvin.
>
> I wanted to hear you say you wished you would have married your high school sweetheart sooner. That lifelong commitment is better than indiscriminate pleasure seeking. I would have liked to have seen you cry for the child your wife bears, who won't have a daddy to grow up with. I would have liked to have heard you admit what our world is forever denying: That we live in a moral universe with moral absolutes that sooner or later judge those who break them.
>
> Instead, you have chosen to become a safe sex spokesman. You're going to tell kids to do something you didn't do. Use a condom. Hasn't anyone told you, Earvin, that a condom doesn't always work? That it will fail the user a certain percentage of times. That you're playing HIV roulette. Years from now, hasn't it occurred to you there may be a number of boys and girls — adults then — hospitalized with bleeding cancerous sores dripping onto their sheepskin mats, with T.B. in their intestines, with pneumonia covering their lungs and tubes running out of their bodies, blind in both eyes with a ventilator forcing oxygen into their now shrunken, disease-ridden bodies and prolonging only the agony and torture . . . and they will be saying, "but Magic told us it was safe."[2]

Magic reminds me of another man who had it all and fell with a great crash — King Saul, the first king of Israel. He is described in 1 Samuel 9:2, and he sounds a lot like Mr. Basketball:

> And he had a son whose name was Saul, a choice and handsome man, and there was not a more handsome person than he among the sons of Israel; from his shoulders and up he was taller than any of the people.

Saul had the talent and ability. I bet he could slam-dunk with the best. He came out of nowhere and attained Israel's crown. But he, like Magic, violated God's principles and lost it all. First Samuel 13:13-14 tells us:

> And Samuel [the prophet] said to Saul, "You have acted foolishly; you have not kept the commandment of the Lord your God, which He com-

manded you, for now the Lord would have established your kingdom over Israel forever. But now your kingdom shall not endure. The Lord has sought out for Himself a man after His own heart, and the Lord has appointed him as ruler over His people, because you have not kept what the Lord commanded you."

It doesn't matter how successful or popular you are by the world's standards; if your heart is not right, life bypasses you. Think of Howard Hughes, once the richest man in the world. He became a paranoid schizophrenic and had isolated himself when he died. Or Marilyn Monroe, the greatest sex queen who ever lived, wife of movie moguls, baseball legends, and mistress to a President, who loved life so much she killed herself.

These people, and those like them, illustrate a fundamental truth about life: You can perfect all the superficial personality traits and achievement skills of worldly success, but if you ignore the integrity of the heart, you will fail. Instead, permanent success in life starts with a heavy-duty heart.

Therefore, in child raising, we must avoid today's common problem of focusing exclusively on the child's personality, behavior, and skills without concentrating on the integrity of the heart. The case studies above demonstrate the folly of the personality cult. When we speak of teaching children, we need to begin with the topic of heart development before moving to personality, behavior, and skills.

I use the term *teach,* the first component in the Equipping process, to convey the idea of transferring the mysteries of *being* and *doing* to the next generation. Fatherhood helps a child develop a heart of integrity and the capacity to be capable (able).

This chapter tells how to lay the foundation for teaching by establishing a stable, learning, perceptive, and wise heart. The next chapter tackles the practical details and presents examples on how to teach children.

In spite of your best intentions, you cannot make a child's heart right. You can't make a child good, wise, righteous, holy, or obedient. Only the child can make a sequence of choices throughout the maturing process that leads to these qualities. All you can do is create the best possible environment and offer guidance that encourages the child to select wisely. God has made the human heart a self-programmer. The heart programs its own destiny. Therefore, your task is to help the child recognize, prefer, and adopt the right "heart-ware."

A child needs to develop an unchangeable deep inner core of being to flex with the outrageous slings and arrows of misfortune. A strong heart has two dimensions: It possesses and it pursues. A strong heart possesses the tranquility of having deep psychological and emotional needs met (a stable heart), and it pursues truth and wisdom.

A STABLE HEART

The more stable the heart, the more able to flex, be creative, and take risks. The more shaky the heart, the more rigid, sterile, and fearful are the responses to life's changing demands.

By the term *stable heart* I mean the inner core of a person that makes up their *being,* and that is rock solid and gives the person depth, resilience, and stamina. This heart condition exists when the four basic psychological needs are met. These needs, the corresponding Four Fatherhood Functions that help produce them, and the component of Christianity that enhances them, are shown in Figure 9.

FOUR FATHERHOOD FUNCTIONS & THEIR BENEFITS	
Love	Significance
Bond	Belongingness
Lead	Identity
Equip	Competence

Figure 9

Love, bond, and lead were covered in Volume 2, *Dad the Family Counselor.* This volume deals with equipping, which develops competence. The father starts the task by performing the fatherhood functions with excellence, which gives the child the best possible chance to write the healthy "heart-ware," producing significance, belongingness, identity, and competence. Then, when the child becomes a Christian, God, Christ, the Holy Spirit, and the church take over, and then correct and reinforce the right "heart-ware."

A LEARNING HEART

Life belongs to the learners. A learning heart has the best chance for survival in a rapidly changing environment. In hazardous times, it may come down to the survival of the fittest, and the least adaptable will be culled. You can't teach a child everything, so the best bet is to cultivate a child to learn to do whatever it takes to survive and flourish.

The world of tomorrow will be different from anything we can even imagine. So how can we teach our children to face it? Think of the parents of the 1890s as they perched on the threshold of the twentieth century and prepared their children for the era of peace they expected during the coming golden age. Think of the wars, the political changes, the technological changes, and the social changes of the twentieth century. Now, here we are perched on the brink of the twenty-first century. What military, social, economic, medical, technological, and political changes will our children have to face? How can we possibly know what to prepare them for? The best thing we can do for our children is to teach them how to cope with change.

According to H. Stephen Glenn, "Human knowledge in our culture is expanding at the rate of 100 percent every five years. In some fields a 100 percent gain in new knowledge every eleven months is not unusual. Many futurists project that if these trends continue, (by the year 2002) graduates will have to be equipped to handle a 100 percent knowledge explosion every thirty-eight days."[3]

What future economic conditions will my children face? I think of Helen and Brandon and the support for a number of retired baby boomers, government workers, and welfare recipients that will have to come out of their paychecks, not to mention foreign aid and our deficit roduction. The takers are growing in number and the makers are dwindling. Will my children be able to produce enough wealth to carry that kind of burden and enjoy a decent standard of living?

The best thing is to give them the basic principles, meet their needs, and free them up to become professional lifetime learners. That's the only way they will stay on the cutting edge and face the problems in a future that we can never imagine. Eric Hoffer says it in this way:

> In times of change, learners will inherit the earth, while the learned
> find themselves beautifully equipped to deal with a world that no long-
> er exists.[4]

With these cataclysmic changes looming on the horizon that will require ever more resourcefulness and ingenuity on the part of our children to handle, we get news of how our educational system gets

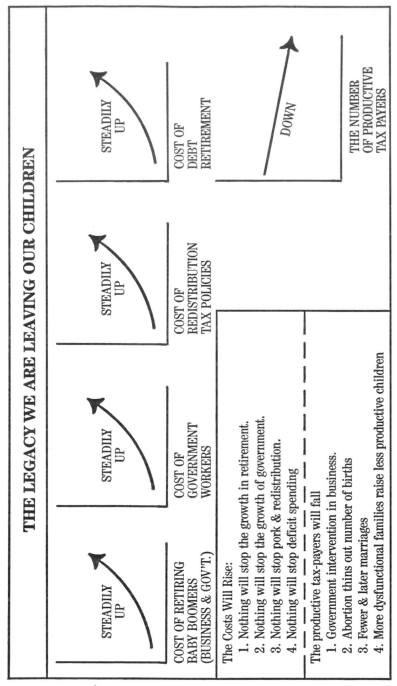

THE LEGACY WE ARE LEAVING OUR CHILDREN

COST OF RETIRING
BABY BOOMERS
(BUSINESS & GOV"T.)
STEADILY UP

COST OF
GOVERNMENT
WORKERS
STEADILY UP

COST OF
REDISTRIBUTION
TAX POLICIES
STEADILY UP

COST OF
DEBT
RETIREMENT
STEADILY UP

THE NUMBER
OF PRODUCTIVE
TAX PAYERS
DOWN

The Costs Will Rise:
1. Nothing will stop the growth in retirement.
2. Nothing will stop the growth of government.
3. Nothing will stop pork & redistribution.
4. Nothing will stop deficit spending

The productive tax-payers will fall
1. Government intervention in business.
2. Abortion thins out number of births
3. Fewer & later marriages
4. More dysfunctional families raise less productive children

Figure 10

36

worse every year. The family, the instrument that prepares children for school, gets worse every year. Our graduates score lower and achieve less every year.

If we turn out fewer children who are going to be less productive but have to support more people in tougher times, what do you see for their future? What implications do these thoughts have on your fatherhood style? One of your major goals in life ought to be to produce children who never stop learning.

A PERCEPTIVE HEART

Learning is a process that starts before birth and never ends. A baby is a learning machine with a voracious appetite for sensory impressions to gain insight into life. Learning by itself, however, is only part of the success process. It behooves a child not just to learn, but more importantly, to learn the right stuff. Indiscriminate learning can cause fatal problems.

Worldview

Children can learn horrible behavior patterns as well as successful ones. We all know young children with behavior disorders who seem to have learned a way of thinking, feeling, and behaving that works against them rather than for them. If I think a person is against me, I will perceive every act as a threat. If I think I am a defective no-good furball, my "perception lens" will filter out the good things about me, and I will see only the stupid mistakes that reinforce my poor self-image.

1. The world is a horrible, or good, place to be.
2. I am an undesirable person and deserve to be rejected, or I am a worthy, honorable person and deserve to be accepted.
3. People hurt me so I keep my distance, or people nurture me so I get close to them.
4. Relationships turn out painful so I avoid them, or relationships comfort me so I pursue them.

Little Gary, five years old, desperately needed playmates, but none of the kids would take a chance on him. They always paid a price to play with Gary. He hit, bit, and verbally abused children until he ran them off. Then he would whine for companionship. The goal in life of seven-year-old Betty was to accumulate everything for herself. She stole, lied, cheated, and manipulated her family and friends to build up her capital base. Her life centered on her things. Sally was a clinger. She draped herself on her mother and wouldn't let go. If her mother put her down, Sally pitched fits. Stanley was an attention addict. His volume increased until only he could be heard. He screamed at swimming pools, yelled in school, bellowed at mealtime, and shrieked in between. He laughed loud, cried long, and talked incessantly.

Since these children all have basic needs that have not been met, in desperation they are performing in extreme ways in a vain attempt to stop the pain. There seems to be some parts in the mind that were placed in backward. If they want love, they should act lovable, not hateful. When they need playmates, they should be friendly, not antagonistic. What and how do kids learn to get their signals crossed up so much?

The problem arises from the worldview the child picks up. Most authorities agree that a baby establishes a basic worldview by age two with many of the details added by age five. A worldview is a basic impression about the nature of life. It is a cluster of perceptions about justice, values, fairness, and the dynamics of relationships. A worldview determines the thoughts, feelings, and behaviors of a child.

In his book, *The 7 Habits of Highly Effective People*, Stephen R. Covey discusses worldview using the term *paradigm*, which he defines as a frame of reference. He explains worldviews as maps:

> A simple way to understand paradigms is to see them as maps. We all know that "the map is not the territory." A map is simply an explanation of certain aspects of the territory. That's exactly what a paradigm is. It is a theory, an explanation, or model of something else. . . . Each of us has many, many maps in our head, which can be divided into two main categories: maps of the way things are, or realities, and maps of the way things should be, or values. We interpret everything we experience through these mental maps.[5]

A baby starts the map-drawing process at birth, and the maps begin to affect all subsequent maps that the baby draws. How the baby does that depends on how his or her existing maps interpret new information. No one records pure truth and reality on his or her maps. Instead, they record their *perceptions* of truth and reality. H. Stephen Glenn writes:

We sometimes believe that what we see determines what we think, but the opposite is true. What we think determines what we see.[6]

Heart-Ware

The baby gathers exhilarating stimuli from personal relationships and programs it into the heart like software into a computer. I call these perceptions written into the heart personal "heart-ware." The "heart-ware" functions at both ends — the data receiving end and the behavior forming end. "Heart-ware" becomes a unique "perception lens" through which the incoming data from the world is seen, shaped, and used to confirm the "heart-ware." On the other end, the "heart-ware" dictates much of our thoughts, feelings, and behaviors (Figure 11).

"HEART-WARE" DETERMINES LIFESTYLE

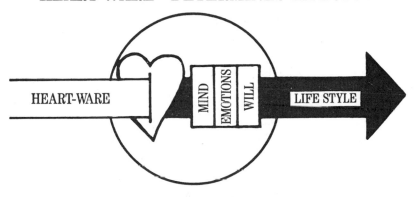

Figure 11

No one sees the world as it really is. We all see it after its image is filtered through our "perception lens." Obviously, success in life is directly related to how close to truth/reality our "heart-ware" is. The more accurate the "heart-ware," the more objective the person and the better the input into all their opinions and decisions. The more distorted the "heart-ware," the more subjective the person and the less dependable the data they use to govern life. The subjective person has unrealistic "heart-ware" that wrecks the natural flow through the mind, emotions, and will, which results in foolish, unprofitable behavior (Figure 12).

Unfortunately, the baby cannot easily discern truth from error or good from bad and often ends up with a distorted defective world-

FLAWED PERCEPTION AND DISTORTED "HEART-WARE" CAUSE BEHAVIOR PROBLEMS

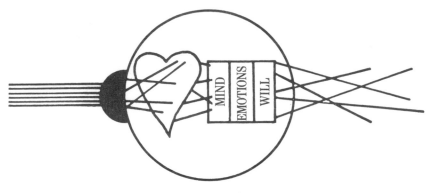

Figure 12

view that damages the heart and impairs behavior for the rest of life. The child can take in horrible input and print it on the heart as true and right.

There are thousands of ways this can happen: the father who shows his daughter child porno and convinces her that it is OK to do it; the mother who tries to get attention needs met from her children because her husband neglects her; the child who is forced to answer the phone and lie for the parents; the child who is forced to win at any cost; the daughter who is forced into talent and beauty contests where exterior beauty is worshiped; and parents who try to relive their frustrated childhoods through their children.

Dysfunctional families produce dysfunctional "heart-ware." Dysfunctional "heart-ware" causes damaging behaviors. Children can get things so twisted that everything starts working backward and they drive away the ones they love. Since babies cannot make the correct connections between their behavior and the pain it brings, they place all the fault in life on others. Since they cannot see cause and effect, they have a perception problem. When "heart-ware" smells, behavior stinks.

In my life, I have been cursed because I have a very distorted "heart-ware" program written into me. My dad (a tall commanding army officer) called me "Stupe" (short for stupid) and told me I would "never amount to anything" for the eighteen years I lived at home. He convinced me. Since he broadcasted a negative destructive message to me all those years, I converted it into a "heart-ware" program and printed it directly onto my heart. My worldview or "map" had me as a seriously defective, shameful failure whom no one could like. Since I did not feel significant, competent, and valuable, I had a grave problem with my identity.

I would have undoubtedly gone on to self-destruct if I had not experienced a major "heart-ware" rewrite. An event happened that changed the course of my life and put me on the way to recovery. This dramatic shift of my worldview is what Stephen R. Covey calls a major paradigm shift. He illustrates how a new way of looking at things can change our lives with this popular story told to Frank Koch in *Proceedings — United States Naval Institute.*

Two battleships assigned to the training squadron had been at sea on maneuvers in heavy weather for several days. I was serving on the lead battleship and was on watch on the bridge as night fell. The visibility was poor with patchy fog, so the captain remained on the bridge keeping an eye on all activities.

Shortly after dark, the lookout on the wing of the bridge reported, "Light, bearing on the starboard bow."

"Is it steady or moving astern?" the captain called out.

Lookout replied, "Steady, Captain," which meant we were on a dangerous collision course with that ship.

The captain then called to the signalman, "Signal that ship: We are on a collision course, advise you change course 20 degrees."

Back came a signal, "Advisable for you to change course 20 degrees."

The captain said, "Send: I'm a captain, change course 20 degrees."

"I'm a seaman second class," came the reply. "You had better change course 20 degrees."

By that time the captain was furious. He spat out, "Send: I'm a battleship. Change course 20 degrees."

Back came the flashing light, "I'm a lighthouse."

We changed course.[7]

Switched Life

The event that helped me reprogram my "heart-ware" happened when I was a junior at Georgia Tech. I first heard the truth about the existence of God, His fatherly concern for us, and what He had done to make it possible for us to know Him and relate to Him in a personal way. He sent Jesus Christ to pay the death penalty for our sins and set up the plan in which we could have Jesus start living inside our hearts. I trusted Jesus Christ as my Savior, and God, my new Father, adopted me into His family and began the long process of reparenting me. (For the complete explanation of my conversion experience, please see chapter 3 of *Dad the Family Coach*.)

The Bible describes this process as dying in Christ and being born again. After my old self died, I became a new person in Christ. I learned through the Scripture that I was now a son of God and that the Spirit of Christ, the Holy Spirit, was now dwelling in me. I now had a solid identity and great significance.

After my conversion experience, I started the process, which all Christians go through, of changing my "heart-ware." Even though I had been born again, my mind still had all the old messages printed on it. I started casting off the "heart-ware" from Dad and putting in the new "heart-ware" from God. And now, years later, I still process the truth from God through my heart and continue my healing.

Paul describes the process in this way:

> Do not conform any longer to the pattern of this world, but be transformed by the renewing of your mind (Rom. 12:2, NIV).

The truth from the Bible provides the source of wisdom that can heal your heart and help you conform your behavior to a manner pleasing to God. You as Dad the Family Shepherd must make this major lifetime heart shift if you expect to lead your children spiritually.

Your children are born learners, but they may learn all the wrong things deep in their hearts where it really counts. You must fulfill your role in guiding them to the truth, wisdom, and freedom that are in Christ.

A WISE HEART

Learning is not enough. A wise heart seeks wisdom. If learning is a hunt, wisdom is the prey.

Children need to learn healthy "heart-ware." "Heart-ware" is another name for wisdom. Children must learn wisdom, the correct view of truth/reality, and the correct understanding of the laws of cause and effect. Wisdom is the canon of eternally true principles that explain reality and govern morality.

Wisdom Learned

Learning is a hunt for wisdom, and people find it in different measure. Wisdom appears in people in many shades: No one is all black or all white. Some people enjoy a lucid view of reality while others gaze through a lens darkly. The closer your "heart-ware" fits truth/reality, the more wisdom you have. The greater the mismatch between your "heart-ware" and truth/reality, the more foolish, blind, and out of touch you are.

The more accurate your "heart-ware," the closer you operate to reality. The world of reality and eternal principles is represented in Figure 13 by the large circle; the small circle represents your understanding of the real world—your map or "heart-ware." The more of reality/truth contained in your "heart-ware," the wiser you are; the less, the more foolish.

Where does wisdom come from? Where can your children pick it up?

Wisdom Appointed

God created a real cosmos consisting of physical properties (matter and energy), and governed by laws of physics, metaphysical beings (such as angels), and principles of life. An absolute God created an absolute world run by absolute principles that exist apart from humans and our time/space/matter/energy continuum. All people interact and cope with the physical world, but the spiritual world remains a mystery to many because there are no human biological senses that intercept and interpret data from the spiritual world.

Input from the spiritual world must be attained by other means. It is something that must be believed to be seen. This data comes to us by faith in the revelation that God painstakingly provided for us: the Bible. The Bible traces for us the source and nature of the true unchangeable principles of reality:

> I, wisdom, dwell together with prudence; I possess knowledge and discretion. . . . Counsel and sound judgment are mine; I have understanding and power. . . . The Lord possessed me at the beginning of His work, before His deeds of old; I was appointed from eternity, from the beginning, before the world began (Prov. 8:12, 14, 22-23, NIV).

The wisdom that God appointed covers two dimensions that fathers must help children master. Children need to learn the truth about the world and about humanity.

1. The world—the truth about the way the world is and the way it works.

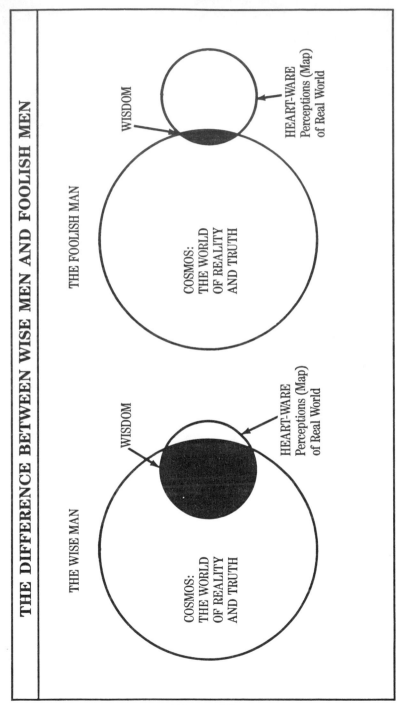

Figure 13

2. Humanity—the truth about what is right and wrong and the laws of cause/effect or behavior/consequences.

Truth includes not only the neutral facts about the world but also the moral and ethical laws that God established to govern human relationships.

Tragically, there are two opposing wisdom clusters: one from God, which is true; and the other from the world, which is false even if it sports imposing credentials. The Bible warns us of the dangerous input of the latter because it abounds and is easily ingested by unsuspecting children.

> Where is the wise man? Where is the scholar? Where is the philosopher of this age? Has not God made foolish the wisdom of the world? For since in the wisdom of God the world through its wisdom did not know Him, God was pleased through the foolishness of what was preached to save those who believe (1 Cor. 1:20-21, NIV).

The wisdom of the world is false and creates dangerous "heartware." Fathers, you must do all you can to lead your children to godly wisdom and away from worldly wisdom.

Wisdom Presented

God presents His wisdom to us in several ways. First, when we trust Christ, we get wisdom/truth/reality. Jesus is the Way, the Truth, and the Life. Next, God can give it directly to us. James 1:5 says, "But if any of you lacks wisdom, let him ask of God, who gives to all men generously and without reproach, and it will be given to him."

God also presents His wisdom through the Scripture:

> The proverbs of Solomon son of David, king of Israel: for attaining wisdom and discipline; for understanding words of insight; for acquiring a disciplined and prudent life, doing what is right and just and fair; for giving prudence to the simple, knowledge and discretion to the young (Prov. 1:1-4, NIV).

God also presents wisdom through fathers:

> My son, pay attention to my wisdom, listen well to my words of insight, that you may maintain discretion and your lips may preserve knowledge (Prov. 5:1-2, NIV).

Wisdom Pursued

Wisdom is readily available: It is presented in a variety of ways. But the other side of acquiring wisdom is the active pursuit of it. A person must desire it, yearn for it, and take initiative for it. The Bible says we must ask God for it and cast about for it:

> My son, if you accept my words and store up my commands within you, turning your ear to wisdom and applying your heart to understanding, and if you call out for insight and cry aloud for understanding, and if you look for it as for silver and search for it as for hidden treasure, then you will understand the fear [awesomeness] of the Lord and find the knowledge of God (Prov. 2:1-5, NIV).

You cannot make a child wise. You can't force-feed wisdom. Each person must reach out and grasp wisdom. We can create only the environment that stimulates the natural desire for wisdom that every child has.

THE REWARD

Developing a child into a seeker of wisdom helps the child, but it also brings great rewards to a father. Helen and Brandon have given me great gratification because of their appreciation for learning and wisdom.

Just before he left to tackle his senior year in college, Brandon approached me and said, "Dad, I need some advice."

"Great, Son, what do you want to know?"

"Well, Dad, I just need some advice."

"I know, Son, but what's the problem?"

"Dad, there is no problem. Can't you just give me some advice?"

"Brandon, what's wrong with you? How can I give advice when I don't know what the problem is?"

"Well, gee, Dad. I am just going off to my last year in college and don't know what all to expect. You have been here before and went through it, and I just wondered if there was something you could tell me that might come in handy."

I realized that Brandon could pay me no higher compliment. He had seen the value of the lessons I had tried to teach him and Helen through the years, and now on the verge of adulthood, he wondered if there was something else he needed to know. The importance of being a lifetime learner had sunk in — and he was still seeking advice from his old man.

E-TEAM HUDDLE GUIDE
CHAPTER ONE: DAD THE FAMILY SAGE

E-TEAM REVIEW
10–15 minutes

Dad, the Family Shepherd
E-TEAM

After coffee and fellowship, allow each man to cover the following:

1. Tell the E-Team your name, occupation, and phone number.

2. Tell the E-Team your wife's name and the names and ages of your children. Record their family information below.

Team Member	His Wife	Phone	Children
1. _____	_____	Of _____ Ho_____	_____
2. _____	_____	Of _____ Ho_____	_____
3. _____	_____	Of _____ Ho_____	_____
4. _____	_____	Of _____ Ho_____	_____
5. _____	_____	Of _____ Ho_____	_____
6. _____	_____	Of _____ Ho_____	_____

E-TEAM DISCUSSION
50–60 minutes

This part allows you to discuss the key concepts in this chapter and relate them to your individual lives. Be sure to leave time to complete the Workout and Encouragement sections.

THE PRINCIPLES (Check the text for help)

1. Discuss why we should make it a priority to cultivate a learning heart in our children.

2. What is "heart-ware" and how does it determine lifestyle?

3. Describe the difference between a wise man and a foolish man as explained by Dave.

THE IMPLICATIONS (Why are these ideas significant?)

4. Fathers play a primary role in developing a learning heart, "heart-ware," and wisdom in a child. There are currently 16 million children without fathers, and 55 percent of the dads who are raising children are dysfunctional. What implications will this have on our society in the next generation?

5. Describe the difference in behavior that you would expect to see between a child who accesses the truth from the spiritual world and a child who has no access to it.

THE APPLICATION (How do these ideas affect me?)

6. How did your dad help or hinder the development of a learning heart in you?

7. What must be true in your life if you expect to transfer biblical "heart-ware" to your children?

E-TEAM WORKOUT
10–15 minutes

Allow each man to choose one of the project options (plays) to perform during the week. If so desired, design your own project. Note: It is essential that each man leave having made a definite commitment to a specific project.

1st PLAY:

Make an appointment with your wife and discuss the concept of "heart-ware" and the diagram in Figure 13.

2nd PLAY:

Make an appointment with each child and find out what he/she believes about God, the Bible, and how one becomes a Christian.

E-TEAM ENCOURAGEMENT
5–10 minutes

Close the meeting in prayer for each other and your families. Include in your prayer a specific request for spiritual power to successfully complete your project.

BREAK THE HUDDLE, GO HOME AND RUN THE PLAY!

Chapter Two
Dad the Family Mentor

TEACH		TRAIN		TRACK		TEND	
1	2	1	2	1	2	1	2

"The human mind, once stretched to a new idea,
never goes back to its original dimensions."
— Oliver Wendell Holmes[1]

FOOTSTEPS

I arose early one morning and took Brandon for a walk across the freshly plowed pasture toward the barn to feed the horses. I walked ahead of him taking long strides to land on the tops of the furrows. I turned to watch the progress of my four-year-old cowboy. Brandon struggled about a dozen rows behind me furiously leaping and floundering, in the knee-high (his knee) barricades of loose dew-wet dirt furrows. He refused to simply step from furrow to furrow. He had to skip every two furrows so his boots would land in his daddy's footsteps. He desperately wanted to walk in his dad's footsteps.

Just to see what would happen, I turned around and walked sideways. When he came to the sideways footprints, he paused, turned sideways, and started crablike across the plowed earth. I walked backward. So did he. I hopped. He hopped. He never looked at me or asked any questions. Undaunted by the extra labor, he soberly pursued his task of copying his father step for step. Brandon did it like Dave. He delighted in my ways.

Can you imagine the glow of warmth in my heart? I reached down and picked up my little cowboy and seated him on my shoulders. I marveled at the display of Father Power in operation. We went on to feed and water the horses, and we had another great father/son episode in our trek through his childhood.

This story shows a child's obsessive learning instinct in action. Our great advantage in producing learners is this: Learners are born, not made. Children are born with an insatiable thirst to learn. All we need to do is let it rip. The problem is not how to start it but how to keep from squelching it. Just keep reinforcing this natural instinct.

This process is what parenting is all about: the transfer of civilization from one generation to the next. Parents play the role of teachers, and children play the role of learners. Perhaps a word that describes the whole process is *absorption:* The new generation absorbs the old one.

DAD THE FAMILY EQUIPPER

Your job in this process has two dimensions: You are Dad the Family Mentor and Dad the Family Minister.

As mentor, you assume the responsibility to provide your children with the education they need. Strong fathers recognize they bear the responsibility for all facets of child education and stay involved in the total process. True, schools have taken the smothering burden of equipping our children with scholastic skills, but you must remember that they function under delegated authority. You are still accountable for your children.

Therefore, you need to be tracking the school carefully and remain actively involved. Make sure that the school has good management and teachers and that the material is acceptable. If not, seek to make changes. If you can't influence the school, change schools even if you must move or pay for private education. How could you do less if you are seriously committed to providing your children with the education they need? Remember the unknown of the twenty-first century and what your children may have to face. This is nothing to play around with.

Strong fathers not only check on schools, they also roll up their sleeves and play a crucial role in each child's study. You need to check the child's learning ability, learning preferences, special interests, learning progress, and learning habits. You should do everything possible to make learning a virtue and priority and to cultivate a good learning environment. You are Dad the Family Tutor.

As minister, your task includes guiding your children along the path to understanding and operating in the security of knowing God through Jesus Christ. Again, you need not perform every detail of this process, but you are responsible to make sure it happens with excellence.

Modular Teaching

Your strategy in this "absorption" process is to broaden the term *teach* to include an assortment of creative methods in a variety of environments over a long period of time. This modular teaching concept formed the backbone of our ministry at Kings Arrow Ranch, a youth camp that Sandy and I founded and directed for many years.

We selected a topical theme for a two-day period and coordinated everything that happened in camp to reinforce the topic we were trying to teach. If the topic was how to develop a servant heart, then our bunkhouse Bible study, the skits at mealtime, the campfire, the personal counseling appointments, and each class would reinforce the topic. The idea came to the children from every direction all day long in a variety of creative ways.

This modular teaching concept comes to us from the Bible. The biblical foundation for how to teach children is Deuteronomy 6:6-9, 20. It commands fathers to teach their children and suggests five basic methods of transferring the truth to the next generation. This chapter covers each of these five teaching methods:

> And *these words*, which I am commanding you today, shall *be on your heart;* and *you shall teach them diligently* to your sons and shall *talk of them* when you sit *in your house* and when you walk by the way and when you lie down and when you rise up. And you shall *bind them as a sign* on your hand and they shall be as frontals on your forehead. And you shall *write them on the doorposts* of your house and *on your gates.* . . . When your son *asks you* in time to come, saying, "What do the testimonies and the statutes and the judgments mean which the Lord commanded you?" (italics added)

TEACH BY MODELING

The Bible puts the pressure on fathers to demonstrate a lifestyle that they want the children to follow: "Give me your heart, my son, and let your eyes delight in my ways" (Prov. 23:26).

The opening story in this chapter about how Brandon walked in my footsteps points out two things:

The good news—your children will copy you.

The bad news—your children will copy you.

BIBLICAL METHODS OF TEACHING		
Method	Verse	Reference
1. Modeling	v. 6	"on your heart"
2. Discussion	v. 7	"teach diligently"
3. Daily Events	v. 7	"talk in your house"
4. Object Lessons	v. 8	"bind them as a sign"
5. Creative Projects	v. 9	"write on your doorposts and on your gates"

Figure 14

The news is good or bad depending on you. Children are natural mimics; they act like their parents in spite of every attempt to teach them good manners. So, you'd better make sure they have something worthwhile to copy. Modeling probably teaches your children more extensively than any other form of teaching. From the time they are born, children act like little duplicating machines. Almost all character and ethical traits are caught, not taught. Children, like blotters, absorb whatever they are dipped into. And, because of Father Power, children are far more apt to copy what you are, not what you say.

Steve Ivaska tells of the lesson on manhood he learned from his father on an afternoon boating trip. His father loaded him into the 12-foot steel boat, put on his life jacket, and shoved away from the dock. As Steve watched his father yank the cord of the old Evinrude, flames flashed out from the back of the boat. An ignition spark had torched a pool of gas that had seeped out of the tank. The next thing Steve knew, he was flying through the air and splashed safely into the lake. With no thought to himself or the boat, his father's first impulse was to save the boy. Then his dad jumped into the water, turned the boat over, and put out the fire. Steve never forgot the lesson on manhood that he had learned from his dad that day: A father thinks of his family first. No lecture would have taught him this as well as the example of his father.

Another father, Dan Lawyer, writes: "As I was playing chase with my little girl, Courtney (20 months old), the arch of my bare foot came down on one of her Duplo Blocks. As I sat on the floor, in pain and rubbing my foot, Courtney walked toward me, looked at my foot and said, 'Owie?' She then got down and kissed my foot. The exciting thing about this is that she not only caught this behavior by watching us kiss her little 'owies' but her little heart was filled with compassion as well."

Modeling. What a powerful tool for conveying wisdom and character traits to children! They will automatically pick up most of their character, social, and communication skills in the process of interacting with you and your wife. Quite simply, they do what you do. Jim Burton confirms this with a report on a survey on how dads affect church attendance:

> When both parents attend Sunday School regularly, 72 percent of the children attend when grown. When just the father attends, 55 percent of the children attend when grown. When only the mother attends, 15 percent of the children attend when grown. When neither parent attends, 6 percent of their children attend when grown. Though related to Sunday School, the survey's message is clear—your children and grandchildren need you to model Christianity for them. The greatest sermon your child will ever hear will be preached by your life of faithfulness in word and deed.[2]

Modeling is the most effortless method of teaching, but, in one major way, it is the most demanding. You must invest vast quantities of time with your children. They can't copy what they don't see. They need to be exposed to you in all kinds of life situations: work, recreation, worship, social settings, emergency and crisis situations, embarrassing occasions, in victory and in defeat. They need someone to step across the furrows and ditches and leave footprints for them to follow. They need you to walk them through life. If you don't model for them, who will?

TEACH BY DISCUSSION

> My son, do not forget my teaching, but let your heart keep my commandments; for length of days and years of life, and peace they will add to you (Prov. 3:1-2).

When you gather yourself up to teach your child, remember that the lecture or sermon style of explaining truth to them has the least success. The more you can capture the feel of informal natural chatting, the better off everybody is. You want to get them asking questions and always leave them wanting more.

Talking to small children often seems unrewarding at the time, but they tuck your words away in their hearts, and the Holy Spirit can bring them to bear on their lives when they need them. Teaching is also one of the biggest faith activities I know of. And yet, planting Scripture (the wisdom of life) in the heart of a child is essential if you expect the child to enjoy any peace through the difficult days and turbulent years of life.

Deuteronomy 6:6-7 reveals three principles of learning that will help you improve your teaching abilities: "And *these words,* which I am commanding you today, shall *be on your heart;* and *you shall teach them diligently* to your sons" (italics added).

Teach the Word

Verse 6 says "these words," which refer to the Scriptures. You are Dad the Family Priest and must convey to your children the truth about God as contained in the Scriptures. "All Scripture is God-breathed and is useful for teaching, rebuking, correcting and training in righteousness, so that the man of God may be thoroughly equipped for every good work" (2 Tim. 3:16, NIV).

Know It in Your Heart

Verse 6 also says, "These words ... shall be on your heart." The word must reside in your heart, and, if it doesn't manifest itself in your life, you have nothing to transfer. Dr. Howard Hendricks says it well: "You cannot impart what you do not possess."[3]

If the truth is not in your heart, you can only talk about it, and it will not show up in your nonverbal signals. Given a choice, a child will always believe the nonverbal communication more than words.

Puncture Them with Truth

The word *diligence* means to sharpen, to assail, to wound, or to pierce with enthusiasm. You must shape and fashion the teaching in such a way that it has enough puncture power to spear the heart. This requires careful thought with the emphasis on learning, not teaching; the learner, not the teacher.

"Teach with diligence" also means to keep teaching consistently, without ever giving up. *Diligence* means to practice regularly or to teach daily. It is also an athletic term that means to continue to compete against overwhelming outside force while struggling with intense inside pain. When the going gets tough, the tough keep teaching. You do whatever it takes to subject your children to consistent dedicated teaching on a regular basis. This means, men, that you may need to cut back on your work schedule or quit playing golf on your day off. We are talking sacrificial teaching here.

COACHING TIPS ON
HOW TO TEACH

1. *Help children see themselves as learners.* The key to developing learners is to establish the idea in children that they were born to learn. That's what they do for a living. You feed, clothe, and shelter them so that they might be about the business of becoming learners. They gaze into your eyes as mirrors and see *learner;* and presto! They see themselves as learners.

H. Stephen Glenn says it this way:

> Our first task as educators is to be sure that the learning environment fosters in students perceptions of themselves as capable, effective human beings. Unless we do so, we will have no effect on our students on the level at which learning takes place.[4]

2. *Establish a learning environment of love and acceptance.* The child must feel that you love him or her on a nonperformance basis. Rudolph Dreikurs wrote: "Until I can risk appearing imperfect in your eyes, without fear that it will cost me something, I can't really learn from you."

Learning requires trust and trust requires friendship. Abraham Lincoln said, "Before you can convince men of anything, you must convince them that you are their friend." (Convention notes: Bobb Biehl)

3. *Conform your expectations to the child's level of performance.* Don't expect a child to do the impossible; settle for limited objectives. If the child knows he or she will fail you, he or she won't take the risk to learn.

4. *Be aware of attention span.* A child can concentrate intently for about seven seconds. That's why all TV cartoons change the scene or action at least every seven seconds. Otherwise, the children get bored and distracted. You must keep things speeding. If you want to wax eloquent on the thread of the Palestinian covenant throughout the Old Testament and debate whether or not it supports covenant or dispensational theology in the pseudepigrapha, fine: Just realize you are teaching patience, not biblical principles.

5. *Be careful of terminology.* You never know what certain terms mean to children.

When Brandon was around four years old, he developed *leeg*-*ophobia*. He became deathly afraid of water *leegs*. Every time he went near the pool, creek, lake, and especially the ocean, he whimpered about the *leegs*, who were going to suck him under the water with giant arms. We tried everything to help him overcome these panic attacks. We were perplexed about *leegs* because none of us had ever heard of a *leeg*, much less seen one. When we asked Brandon to describe them, they sounded like gigantic creatures from the Black Lagoon. Where did he become frightened of *leegs?*

About five years later, our family stayed up to watch the late movie, and Brandon broke out in hysterical laughter. He had solved the mystery of the baffling *leegs*. We were watching a gut-wrenching scene of men being sucked and eaten by a giant underwater monster with big arms and a huge beak. The monster was a giant squid, and the movie was *Twenty Thousand* Leegs *Under the Sea.* There were 20,000 of those nasty *leegs* out there, and Brandon just knew that Ole Captain Nemo let a few get away. And who knows where they might surface next?

6. *Use word pictures.* Why do you suppose Aesop's Fables were so successful in teaching principles? Why did old English fairy tales teach so many generations of British children? Why do the stories of Brer Rabbit communicate principles so well? Why are proverbs so profound? Because they all use word pictures to communicate on an emotional level as well as an intellectual level. Emotions drive truth deep into little hearts.

7. *Celebrate achievement: Don't berate failure.* Beware of the old glass-of-water dilemma: Is it half empty or half full? Did the child accomplish half or fail half? Take the successful half and go bananas.

8. *Reward curiosity, analysis, and experimentation.* Encourage questions. Play detective with them. Give them problems to solve and broken things to fix. Let them get out of problems and then analyze the situation with them. Leave them wanting more: Don't tell them to death. Common errors are to lecture too long and explain too much. Let them experience the thrill of the hunt and discovery and solution.

9. *Allow for learning style and preference.* Some children are verbal learners; some learn best with graphics and pictures; some learn by experience and doing; and some won't learn until they fail. Some love parables; others just the facts. Some like learning bursts with

long periods of consolidation; some like consistent little bite-size learning morsels. Some can gear up to learn only under pressure and enjoy cramming; others cannot learn at all with any pressure. You must discover and respect your child's learning preference, or your efforts will accomplish the opposite of what you intend.

10. *Promote teamwork learning.* Do things as a team. All of life is a series of teamwork situations except the artificial scholastic model where you memorize and are tested individually. Life occurs on a team, and teams working together foster exciting learning habits.

11. *Dialogue with the child.* Make appointments, schedule family meetings, and talk off the cuff with the child to find out what they are learning. Make "What did you learn?" one of the most common phrases in your home.

12. *Do case studies.* Take real people and characters in stories and make them into case studies. Study their actions and behavior and discover the principles of cause and effect. Teach the children the laws of consequences. Ask them to analyze how people get into and out of trouble. How do people insulate themselves from trouble? What are the common habits of winners?

13. *Establish the home as a learning environment.* Make bookshelves, toys, games, and hobbies a prominent feature in your decor. Don't try to make your home into an immaculate sterile *Better Homes and Gardens* model when you have little learners scouring the terrain looking for something to learn. Put the TV and music center in an inconspicuous place to minimize its attraction.

TEACH BY DAILY EVENTS

In Deuteronomy 6:7, it says, *"You shall teach them diligently* to your sons and shall *talk of them* when you sit *in your house* and when you walk by the way and when you lie down and when you rise up"* (italics added). This means you should take the natural opportunities that come up around the home on an ordinary day to pass along biblical truth and wisdom.

Helen and Brandon were both home sick with the flu and watching TV in a typical cartoon trance. This particular winter morning, they were lying in their sleeping bags and playing with a new batch of about a half-dozen baby rabbits during the commercials. Brandon, six years old, went to the bathroom. When he came back, his favorite cartoon came on. He dashed into the room and leaped on his sleeping bag . . . which covered a baby rabbit.

The little bunny let out a shrill scream and went into convulsions. Brandon screamed in fright and anguish. Sandy rushed in. She found Brandon sobbing over and over, "I killed it." She took the dying bunny out back and finished it off. She came back, picked up her boy, and just held him in her lap and comforted him.

That afternoon, when he calmed down and could listen, she stretched out with him on the bed and just talked for a while. She carefully brought up the subject of the bunny, "Brandon, I'm sorry about what happened this morning. I know you are too." She went on to comfort and soothe him. Then she asked, "Brandon, do you remember how you felt when it happened?"

"Yes," he replied.

"You know that strong emotion that you felt?" she asked. "Do you know what that's called?"

"You mean when I felt guilty?" Brandon answered.

"Yes." Sandy went on, "Well, you remember how unpleasant it felt? How miserable you were?" Brandon did. "Well, I want you to think about something. That bad feeling you had is like what Jesus felt when He was on the cross. Except He felt a thousand times worse because He felt the sins of all the people in the world. He actually felt the guilt of the whole world. And He died for all of us. Brandon, he did all of that because He loves you so much. He forgave us for all the wrong things we ever do. You are forgiven. Now the hard thing for you will be to forgive yourself."

Brandon, a six-year-old boy, grasped the meaning of the cross in a unique new way. He sensed a particle of the great suffering our Savior and Lord endured on the cross on our behalf. All because of a sad accident with a baby rabbit. Sandy was there and alert to take advantage of an opportunity that came up around the home to teach a difficult theological truth to her boy.

Picture your children as baby birds in a nest with their mouths gaping open groping for a morsel from mama bird. These are teachable mouths.

TEACH BY OBJECT LESSONS

Deuteronomy 6:8 says, "You shall *bind them as a sign* on your hand and they shall be as frontals on your forehead" (italics added). I interpret this sentence to suggest that you should always be alert for teaching illustrations. Keep the biblical principles at your fingertips and on the top of your mind just waiting to leap out for your children. Your lessons should lie crouching beneath the surface and straining to capture your kids. Equipped with the truth, you lie in wait, seeking those opportune, impressionable moments.

We use this method in every class and activity at Kings Arrow Ranch. For instance, during the first class of riflery, the instructor teaches the safety precautions, the firing procedure, and then gives a demonstration. Earning great respect for a few bull's eyes, he lowers the rifle as if something is wrong.

A hush steals over the whole range. He gathers full attention. Then, he says, "I'm going to shoot one more bull's eye To hit the center of the target, my sights have to be perfectly focused If they are sighted in, I'll hit it. If they are off just a little, by the time the bullet gets down there, it might miss the whole target. That's because of a principle in geometry: Error increases with distance.

"This principle works in your spiritual life as well," he continues. "Even though you have Christian parents and go to a good church, your sights might be off. By the time you get to high school or college, you might not believe anything anymore and miss the whole target and go off the deep end. Your sights need to be focused perfectly on a personal relationship with Jesus Christ if you expect to be on target by the time you graduate from college."

Do you think those kids learned that principle? In fact, it communicates to you right now as you read this story. Think how it hit those kids. They are down at the rifle range and smell the pungent cordite, gun smoke, and pine sap from the woods. And they get to shoot next. They are primed for learning.

The principle behind object lessons is that you can take something familiar and easy to understand and use it to teach a more difficult abstract concept. Jesus taught His disciples in this way. He constantly referred to agricultural and economic stories to drive home His points. Think of the four soils, the mustard seed, mending nets, catching fish, Roman coins, lost sheep, grapevines, fig trees, and the good Samaritan.

A good family shepherd finds hundreds of everyday things to use as object lessons. Wrap up your spiritual truths in tasty parcels and cast them into those baby bird mouths while you can. Play on their unbounded curiosity and voracious appetites. Remember, the early bird gets the baby birds to swallow the worm.

TEACH BY CREATIVE PROJECTS

Deuteronomy 6:9 says, "And you shall *write them on the doorposts* of your house and on your gates" (italics added). This suggests to me that you should think of creative ways around the home to keep the Word before you and the children. Here are some coaching tips on how to do this.

Teach with Play

Children love to play and be entertained. Use puppets, crayons, pipe cleaners, finger paint, Legos™, and other toys. Use games. There is a great selection of Bible-oriented games now available. One of our favorites is Bible Trivia. Make up your own methods.

Sandy and I took the cardboard box our washer came in and cut a TV screen out of it. I got down on my bad football knees and acted out stories for our children. The kids soon learned to come up and change the channel, and instantly I had to act out another story. (This got old fast.) Afterward, we would ask the children what lessons they had learned that would help their spiritual lives.

Teach with Animals

All children love fluffy cuddly little animals. A small pet will naturally bring out the nurturing instincts of a child.

A pet brings out the servant attitude of love. A child soon learns that pets require sacrifice. Animals make great teaching aids because the consequences affect life, health, and death. Giving a child the responsibility for a little life will teach lessons that nothing else will. The proper care and feeding of pets and animals teach responsibility, consistency, and dependability. Feeding is not like studying; you can't put it off for a few weeks and then cram the night before the test. See how they like cleaning cages and removing wastes. The child gets the picture quickly that love demands service.

Recent research has shown that animal care makes good therapy for troubled children, especially a large dog or horse. The hugeness of the animal increases the feeling of importance and, therefore, the value of the primary caregiver. A child feels this: "Look how great my pet is! It demands my attention. If I take care of it, I'll get a lot of value out of it."

Teach on Felt Needs

Brandon and I embarked on a joint project the summer he graduated from high school. He decided he wanted to get several of his graduating friends together with their dads to study an E-Team course I had just written called "The Male Friendship Course." He thought of it, called all the men, scheduled it, and managed it. I only lectured and led the discussion. It proved to be a great help to the boys, who went off to college and started building friendships that will last a lifetime. But the project also taught Brandon a lot about organizing and managing a small-group Bible study.

Teach with Tales

Fill 'em up with stories. Children are fascinated with good stories. Sandy started out reading stories to the kids before they could even talk. She knew they could enjoy the pictures and the expressions in her voice and on her face. They also understood more words than we thought. Sandy read to them almost every night for years. After every story she asked questions and brought out useful lessons. Through her reading, she taught them wisdom (cause and effect) that they could apply in their lives.

I picked up on this when they were older and read the entire Illustrated Bible to them. There were six volumes in the set, and every page had excellent illustrations—it read like a comic book. They studied each picture and listened intently. They gained an incredible understanding of the Bible as a whole as well as learning all the great Bible stories. The Bible contains some of the best stories ever written, and the children really appreciated them.

One day, I heard Brandon singing while he was playing outside. He sang what seemed like one song for about twenty minutes. I discovered he had completely memorized his entire long-playing, Snoopy and the Red Baron record album in just a few days. After Sandy and I rushed right out and bought some Christian records, Helen and Brandon soon saturated their brains with Christian principles through music. Later, we bought a set of tapes that contained the Bible word for word with good music in the background. They still listen to this set driving back and forth from college.

Over a period of three years, I read the entire series of J.R.R. Tolkien's Hobbit books. We used the stories as takeoff points for discussion of "consequence truths" and "cause/effect wisdom."

I invented an epic saga of little deerlike creatures, borrowed every story plot I ever heard, and put Tanyasi and Runnymede in them. Each story had "cause/effect wisdom," which we discussed afterward.

61

Teach with the Publishers

Visit your local Christian bookstore and survey the materials available to help you teach your children. Every family shepherd should be well stocked with an arsenal of books, tapes, records, music, and video products. There is no limit to Christian educational resources available to you. Also, there are many materials available to teach and equip you to use teaching media and become a better instructor. Please, visit the bookstore or church library with your wife.

Teach with Duplication

Teaching is hard work. It takes time, effort, and skill. You need to master these five teaching methods to transfer wisdom and cause/effect laws to your children.

One way to multiply your efforts and improve your effectiveness is to record every devotion and talk you have with your children. Then you can teach them many times over and enhance their learning. When you travel across country on vacation, throw a recorder in the backseat and let them listen to your voice teaching them about life. Your wife can play the tapes for them while you travel.

Think about this: When your children are grown, they can play the tapes for their children, and your grandchildren will hear you teaching their mom or dad and hear their parents' childlike voices asking questions and learning the Word of God. What about your third and fourth generations?

Teach with Efficiency

Probably nothing has done more to dull the learning desire of children than television. Research shows that most children will watch 15,000 to 18,000 hours of TV before they graduate from high school—more time than they will ever spend in a classroom. Not only are the lessons from TV bad, but the hypnotic effect it produces in viewers also kills learning initiative. The writers at *Esquire,* in an article entitled "How to Raise a Perfect Kid," give this report on TV and kids.

> Experts don't just warn about the inherent effects of watching, the passivity it generates, and the restlessness it instills. John Rosemond points out that in watching television, children are not exploring the world, not using their imaginations, not being creative, and not practicing motor skills or hand-eye coordination.[5]

In addition to these negatives about TV, consider that the secular media beams hours of secular-humanism lessons into your home. The industry is saturated with wisdom of the world and a focus on all the wrong "heart-ware" that can damage your children.

At your weekly family meeting, make television activity a portion of your agenda. Have the family select the entire weekly viewing schedule. This agenda enforces the limits and eliminates impulsive viewing.

THE FATHERING DIFFERENCE

Who knows how the life stories of Magic Johnson and King Saul would have been different if they had been exposed to better "heart-ware"? You can make the difference in your children if you fulfill your responsibility to teach them the wisdom and truth that enable them to be true champions in the heart as well as in the field.

E-TEAM HUDDLE GUIDE
CHAPTER TWO: DAD THE FAMILY MENTOR

E-TEAM REVIEW
10–15 minutes

Dad, the Family Shepherd
E-TEAM

> After coffee and fellowship, take 10–15 minutes to allow the men to tell about the results of last week's project. This is the accountability part. Be firm with each other and encourage everyone to complete the projects. If anyone encountered difficulty or had a family problem arise, pause to allow the E-Team to address the problem and pray.

E-TEAM DISCUSSION
50–60 minutes

> This part allows you to discuss the key concepts in this chapter and relate them to your individual lives. Be sure to leave time to complete the Workout and Encouragement sections.

THE PRINCIPLES (Check the text for help.)
1. What is modular teaching?
2. Define the five methods of teaching found in Deuteronomy 6:6-9.
3. Which coaching tip on teaching meant the most to you?

THE IMPLICATIONS (Why are these ideas significant?)
4. Consider the opportunities your child presently has for biblical teaching and determine what percentage of it is lecture and what percentage comprises the other four methods. What are the implications of this?
5. If fathers are responsible for the overall education of their children, what involvement should they have in their schools?

THE APPLICATION (How do these ideas affect me?)
6. Which of these five methods of teaching had the greatest impact in your life when you were a child?
7. Which of these methods do you currently use the most with your children?
8. Which methods do you think you need to improve in and use more often?

E-TEAM WORKOUT
10–15 minutes

Allow each man to choose one of the project options (plays) to perform during the week. If so desired, design your own project. Note: It is essential that each man leave having made a definite commitment to a specific project.

1st PLAY:
Choose one method from this chapter and use it to teach a scriptural principle to each child in your family.

2nd PLAY:
Stop by a Christian bookstore or your church library and evaluate the materials available for children. Select one product for each of your children and follow through: read it or give it to be read. Bring it to the next E-Team meeting and show it to your E-Teammates and rate its effectiveness for them.

3rd PLAY:
Make an appointment with the person in your church who is responsible for children's Christian education and ask about the philosophy, the curriculum, and teaching method currently in use. Report to your E-Team and discuss how you can get involved or supplement your church's youth work.

E-TEAM ENCOURAGEMENT
5–10 minutes

Close the meeting in prayer for each other and your families. Include in your prayer a specific request for spiritual power to successfully complete your project.

BREAK THE HUDDLE, GO HOME AND RUN THE PLAY!

The Fatherhood Function: To Train

Chapter Three
Dad the Family Guide

TEACH		TRAIN		TRACK		TEND	
1	2	1	2	1	2	1	2

*"Highly proactive people . . . do not blame
circumstances, conditions, or conditioning for their
behavior. Their behavior is a product of their own
conscious choice, based on values, rather than
a product of their conditions, based on feeling."*
—*Stephen R. Covey*[1]

HOG WILD
by Helen Simmons
for Freshman Composition Course
Baylor University, 1987

As I look back on my childhood, one incident stands out far above the rest as being unique and unforgettable. My dear, overzealous father was always seeking new opportunities to teach my brother and me responsibility. We had recently moved into a small farming community from the fast-paced city of Dallas. I was in that unstable, junior high time of trying to impress new people into being my friends.

All was going well in my life until one day my little social world crumbled. It was a dreary Monday afternoon when my father sped recklessly into the driveway, pulling a beat-up old trailer.

I ran out to see what he could possibly be hauling in this awful-looking old U-Haul. Inside, two pink baby piglets stared up at me with their beady little eyes. My father gleefully informed me that he had signed my brother and me up in a 4-H Club. We were to raise and train these pigs for six months, and then show them at the county fair.

I was panic-stricken. My father was too excited about his latest scheme to teach us responsibility to hear my faint cries of protest.

For weeks I worried, cried, and tried every way in the world to get out of this. Father remained firm. In fact, he was adamant. My greatest fear was that one of my new junior high friends would somehow find out about this pig show. They would hate me. I didn't know many boys who liked girls with pig manure on their shoes.

For the first five of the six months, my plan of action was to ignore the situation completely. I tried to explain to my dad that since I had refused to enter that smelly old pigpen to train my pig, and since I had paid my little brother off to feed and water my pig, he should just go ahead and sell mine. After all, I wasn't learning about responsibility. He didn't seem to share my views in this area, so the pigs continued to live in our pigpen.

Finally, one day I realized that the show could not be the end of the world. I knew that none of my new friends would be caught dead at a pig show, so there was no danger of being seen. I found great comfort in that thought.

The big day finally arrived all too soon. We unloaded our untrained, dirty, hairy pigs to be shown with all the other trained, clean, shaved pigs. I was not even sure which of the two little beasts was mine.

As I began to look around the show area, horror gripped my stomach. Three of my new junior high friends were all dressed up and heading for the show barn. It was horrible. All of the "in crowd" were there. All of the popular boys were showing cattle or pigs.

I think I tried to run away. Everything was blurry. The human mind has a way of protecting itself from trauma by blocking out horrible experiences, so I do not remember much about the show. I vaguely remember my father picking me up and placing me in the ring behind my pig. I think he was mumbling something about learning a lesson the hard way about responsibility.

I began to regain my memory in the car on the way home. I noticed three large trophies in my lap. My overjoyed father explained that my pig had won the whole show. That, of course, meant that I would have to show my pig at the district fair. I had won a trophy for showmanship, which, ironically, meant that I had the best-trained porker.

I was almost excited about my newfound fame. I did, in fact, get my picture on the front page of the paper. All the junior high kids now worshiped me. I had not realized it before, but pig shows are "big time" in small country towns.

I guess that everything turned out better than I had ever expected. The only problem was that, once again, my father had been right. I learned a lot about responsibility. My dear old dad is always right, and that sure does make me mad.

Rebuttal: by Dave (The Paternal Zealot) Simmons
I never met a kid yet who didn't have his or her character improved after dealing in pig slop. Seriously, if I had it to do all over again, I don't think I would have enrolled my children in "hogdom" without discussing it with them first. But, I made a lot of stupid mistakes in those early years of fathering. That was just when I began to take fathering seriously, and maybe I tilted a little toward fervent fatherhood in my desire to catch up on the task of training my children.

Elusive Training

The good news: Children were born to be trained and much of the process operates automatically.

The bad news: Children start out unable to select good training over bad and pick up whatever they are dished.

More bad news: Child development is infinitely complex and humanity will probably never fully comprehend it.

Some good news: We can understand enough about it to significantly enhance our fathering skills.

Success Training

Training puts the shoes on teaching. If teaching is giving a child a pair of shoes, training puts them on and breaks them in. Training converts the "heart-ware" into behavior.

> Train a child in the way he should go, and when he is old he will not turn from it (Prov. 22:6, NIV).

In this verse, the word *train* means to create a desire for a pleasant mixture of berry paste by putting it on the palate of a child. This gives the child a desire to start eating. In the Book of Hebrews, the term *train* means to exercise vigorously to develop the body and the mind to the place where they should be.

> But solid food [Scripture] is for the mature, who by constant use have
> trained themselves to distinguish good from evil (Heb. 5:14, NIV).

Training, then, is the function in the equipping process that
guides a child through rigorous practice to make moral decisions
and form good habits. Training consists of all those activities that
motivate a child to develop a heart of integrity and cultivate successful patterns of living.

This chapter talks about the elements involved in training: the
man, the tools, and the child. The next chapter deals with the
process of training.

THE MAN

Every team is a reflection of the leader, for good or bad. A corporation, a football team, a military unit, and a family all take on the
characteristics of the man in charge. Therefore, when it comes to
child training, the kind of man you are plays a key role in how your
children will turn out. A successful father makes sure that he walks
with God and models the kind of life he wants his children to
absorb.

Prayerful Training

The closer your children walk with the Lord, the better off they will
be. The more you, Dad the Family Priest, pray for them, the better
their chances are to attain spiritual maturity.

> For this reason also, since the day we heard of it, we have not ceased to
> pray for you and to ask that you may be filled with the knowledge of His
> will in all spiritual wisdom and understanding, so that you may walk in
> a manner worthy of the Lord, to please Him in all respects, bearing
> fruit in every good work and increasing in the knowledge of God (Col.
> 1:9-10).

If Paul and Timothy prayed like this for the brethren in Colossae,
can fathers pray any less for their children? Prayer is God's lever to
make things happen in this world.

Kevin Ring understands the importance of prayer. After the birth
of his second child, his wife was unable to conceive another child
because of medical complications. Kevin prayed, "Please hear my
prayer, O Lord, and make it possible for my wife, Gail, to conceive."
A couple of months later, she announced the coming of a third

little Ring. Kevin continues to pray for all three of his boys "to be godly men who marry godly women and have godly children, and that all the descendants for the next four generations will have hearts that are fully committed to God."

Honorable Training

Children do what you are, not what you say. You must be what you want your children to do. The initial step in training is demonstration and verification. If you put biblical "heart-ware" into practice and it yields positive benefits, your children are apt to follow your steps. Jesus said it in this way: "A student is not above his teacher, but everyone who is fully trained will be like his teacher" (Luke 6:40, NIV).

Modeling puts the child on first base, but it takes a lot more to get the child around the bases to home plate. The child needs to be advanced with explanation, internalization, and practice, but without the father consistently living what he teaches, training won't even get that child to first base.

THE TOOLS

Fathers who excel at work but flounder at home often do so because they know exactly what to do at work while they are confused about their assignment concerning their children at home. A hunter can't hit what he can't see; a father can't do what he doesn't know. When you think of transferring civilization to the next generation or equipping a child to cope with life, what tools do you actually need to make this transfer?

A child needs a set of tools with which to tackle life. These tools will help the child to become capable of coping with life. I have listed these tools and broken them into three categories I call Pneuma (spirit) Tools, Power Tools, and Hand Tools.

With these goals in mind, turn now to the process of training your children to accomplish these goals.

Child training requires that you constantly switch your perspective from the big picture to the tiny detail: You need to see the mountain range but take note of the wild flowers. Keep the overall objectives of child raising in mind but keep a list of short-range goals processing through the agenda. Overtraining or training in too many things simultaneously will burn a child out. So choose your goals carefully and work on them systematically until they are accomplished, then move on to others.

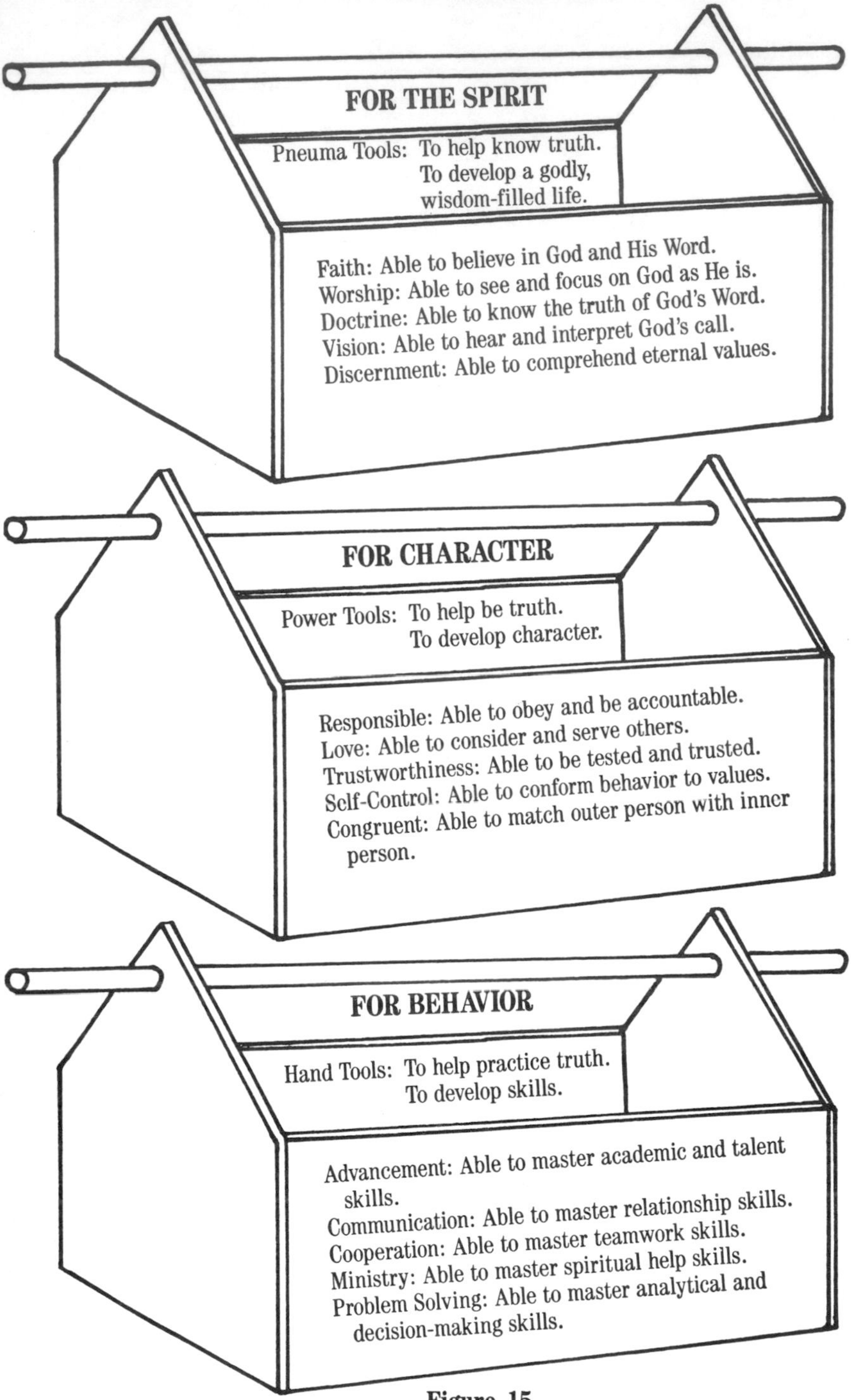

Dad the Family Mentor

FOR THE SPIRIT

Pneuma Tools: To help know truth.
To develop a godly,
wisdom-filled life.

Faith: Able to believe in God and His Word.
Worship: Able to see and focus on God as He is.
Doctrine: Able to know the truth of God's Word.
Vision: Able to hear and interpret God's call.
Discernment: Able to comprehend eternal values.

FOR CHARACTER

Power Tools: To help be truth.
To develop character.

Responsible: Able to obey and be accountable.
Love: Able to consider and serve others.
Trustworthiness: Able to be tested and trusted.
Self-Control: Able to conform behavior to values.
Congruent: Able to match outer person with inner
person.

FOR BEHAVIOR

Hand Tools: To help practice truth.
To develop skills.

Advancement: Able to master academic and talent
skills.
Communication: Able to master relationship skills.
Cooperation: Able to master teamwork skills.
Ministry: Able to master spiritual help skills.
Problem Solving: Able to master analytical and
decision-making skills.

Figure 15

Keep in mind that goals fall into three categories:

1. Being goals: These pertain to the inner person.
2. Doing goals: These pertain to skills and tasks.
3. Habit goals: These pertain to behavior patterns.

Training for each type of goal is different. "Being" goals depend on who you are and what you model: they are mostly caught. "Doing" goals depend on your expertise and understanding of the task: they are mostly taught. "Habit" goals depend on your convictions: they are mostly fought! You must overcome a lot of resistance to help a child develop good habit patterns.

It helps to have these tools and goals in mind as you move through the rest of the training, tracking, and tending phases of equipping your child.

THE CHILD

Running beneath and through all of the tools listed above are a couple of quality traits that are essential to cultivate in your children if you want them to master the issues of life. Children need to develop a responsible heart and a balanced heart. By responsible, I mean they need to develop the capacity to "own" themselves, write their own "heart-ware," and be responsible for their response to life's situations. By balanced, I mean the delicate harmony of being both person-oriented and task-oriented.

Only lately have I been learning these lessons. I have struggled through many personal problems all my life because I have not realized the truth and importance of being responsible and balanced. I wish I had learned these principles of responsibility and balance when I was a child, or at least during my early fatherhood when I could have helped my children absorb them. But I didn't, and I have paid the price.

For example, I landed in Chicago during a winter storm and missed my connection to sunny California. I had to reschedule rapidly because I was to speak at a conference in the evening and could not be late. I checked the monitors and discovered another flight leaving in a few minutes, so I ran through the airport to the ticket counter to get my ticket changed. As I turned the corner to the ticket counter, I ran into an angry mob of hundreds of stranded travelers.

Since the next flight was on another airline, I wasn't sure where to get my ticket changed. To find out, I crowded up to the ticket counter and addressed the harried employee, "May I ask you a question about where to change my ticket?" She glared at me with fire in her eyes and said, "Why don't you get in line like everyone else and take your turn?" I exploded like a clay pigeon on a skeet-shooting range.

In disgust, I bolted to the other airline, got my ticket changed, and barely made my flight. I spent several lovely hours steaming, sizzling, and popping Rolaids at 32,000 feet right over the snow-capped Rocky Mountains. I fumed at the crass response of that woman. It wasn't until the plane began to descend at Los Angeles that I realized that some haggard woman hundreds of miles away had been controlling my mind, my stomach, my blood chemistry, my heart rate, and my spiritual life.

I had turned the controls of my life over to a stranger and given her great power to affect my mind, emotions, will, and behavior. I had transferred responsibility for my life to another. I had acted like a spoiled child, not a responsible adult. My life was governed by extrinsic controls and not by intrinsic principles.

A Responsible Child

The ultimate goal of parenting is to transfer the control of civilization over to the next generation. To this end, our task is to equip our children to maintain and even improve upon the spiritual life, the values, the social order, and the government system that we leave them. Responsibility is the key word. Our goal is to produce responsible people.

A responsible man is a man in control of his life. The process of maturity is going from absolutely no control to control. A responsible man takes charge of his own life. Stephen Covey, in his excellent book, *The 7 Habits of Highly Effective People,* says it better than anyone else:

> Look at the word responsibility — "response-ability: — the ability to choose your response." Highly proactive people recognize that responsibility. They do not blame circumstances, conditions, or conditioning for their behavior. Their behavior is a product of their own conscious choice, based on values, rather than a product of their conditions, based on feeling.[2]

The role parents play in this process is to equip the child to obey. A child learning to obey outside authorities will mature to the point where obedience to internal principles is possible. Parents encourage this behavior by starting with external controls and then guiding the child through the process of developing inner controls. The integrity of the parents and their commitment to the training principles are essential to the success of this process. The job description of the child is simple: learn to obey. The Bible puts it plainly:

> Children, obey your parents in the Lord, for this is right. Honor your father and mother (which is the first commandment with a promise) (Eph. 6:1-2).

One of the Ten Commandments (Ex. 20:12) tells us that children have one duty—to honor parents—and the evidence of this shows up in obedience. Leviticus 20:9 and Deuteronomy 27:16 pronounce a sentence of death upon a son who curses or chronically disobeys his parents. God simply doesn't want His people raising an out-of-control generation. If a high enough percentage of children grow up in any one generation not knowing how to control themselves, that nation will not endure. The parents will have failed in their sacred task of transferring the control of civilization to the next generation.

A man lacking self-control suffers from the AIDS of character traits and success patterns: He has no immunity to the failure viruses that saturate the culture of human activities. Self-control acts as a tool with which to cultivate many of the other important character traits and success patterns. Self-control forms the bedrock of all relationships and civil order. Citizens with little self-control spawn a society of chaos and a life of splintered relationships.

> Like a city that is broken into and without walls is a man who has no control over his spirit (Prov. 25:28).

A responsible man takes ownership of his mind, emotions, and will to effect appropriate behavior. He champions accountability for his own life. A responsible man places life under inner controls based on principles. Feelings and actions are subordinated to an absolute value system. An irresponsible man reacts to life's situations and lets outside factors dictate feelings and behavior. He quickly passes the buck. He avoids accountability.

A responsible man abides by internal determinism; that is, he believes we are proactive individuals and can take responsibility for the issues of life and be held accountable. An irresponsible man abides by external determinism; that is, he believes we are reactive creatures who have little or no control over the issues of life. For a contrast, see Figure 16.

A CONTRAST BETWEEN EXTRINSIC DETERMINISM AND INTRINSIC DETERMINISM	
External Determinism	Internal Determinism
Unresponsible Heart Reactive Person	Responsible Heart Proactive Person
Part of worldly wisdom "Heart-ware" is written for me Others are responsible Others' weaknesses control Makes me a victim I am reactive Life happens to me I transfer problems Happiness depends on others Makes me codependent Results in fatalism Others shepherd me	Part of godly wisdom I write the "heart-ware" I am responsible My strength controls Makes me a leader I am proactive I make life happen I solve problems Happiness depends on me Makes me interdependent Results in hope I shepherd others

Figure 16

1. Extrinsic Determinism is a worldly "heart-ware" map that states: I am *not* responsible for my behavior because I am a product of outside conditioning that predetermines my reactions to life situations.

It says your center of control is on the outside, whether it be genetic design, early family conditioning, people, conditions, or even false "heart-ware" that was lodged in your heart. The bottom line is that you are helpless under the controlling power these outside stimuli have over you. Life happens to you. You are a victim.

These outside forces control your moods, which makes you codependent on others (usually their weaknesses) for your cues on emotions and behaviors. Your happiness or sadness depends on the opinions and acceptance of others and on what is happening to you. This condition usually puts you in performance-based relationships that lead to failure and the formation of a shame-based heart.

These external stimuli have reinforced a false "heart-ware" program, which contains a list of predetermined reactions. Whenever the control buttons are pushed, specific emotions and actions are automatically triggered. It's as if the control factors have bypassed your values, principles, and will and play a program of behavior prescribed for you. Problems and conflicts come to you, damage you, and continue on through you to affect others.

Since you can't seem to control your input or output, soon you adopt a fatalistic approach to life that reinforces your helpless "heart-ware" message. Your perception lens increasingly distorts reality. Your belief in your helplessness becomes a self-fulfilling prophecy, and you are rendered dependent without hope.

Extrinsic determinism dominates our culture, saturates our legal system, and drives our government. It says criminals are not responsible; society is guilty. It says society has wrongly socialized people who commit crimes. It says vast blocks of people cannot be responsible for their own lives. Therefore, the government must provide for them. It says it is not your fault if you get AIDS.

2. Intrinsic Determinism is a godly "heart-ware" map that states: I *am* responsible for my behavior because I am endowed with the ability to choose my response to life situations based on my set of values.

It says your center of control is inside you. You are an independent self-aware being with the ability to override the power of outside stimuli and take control of your responses. You make life happen. You are responsible.

You are endowed with the capacity to subordinate your feelings and behavior to your value system. Your happiness depends on the decisions you make on how to respond to people and conditions. These conditions allow healthy interdependent relationships to develop and lead to mutual respect.

You recognize you are a "heart-ware" programmer and can write a script into your heart based on godly wisdom principles. Whenever external stimuli bombard you, you can push your own buttons and determine your own emotional response and behavior patterns. Problems and conflicts come to you. You solve them and behave with integrity.

As your perception lens focuses more closely on reality and you gain consistent control over your responses to life's situations, you eventually adopt a positive, hopeful approach to life that reinforces your godly wisdom, "heart-ware" message. You grow wiser.

A Balanced Child

A talented child with learning, wisdom, and a high achievement capacity but without a loving and servant attitude is like a hamburger bun without the meat. Where's the beef? A child needs a heart balanced with these human-nurturing qualities.

To have everything except love is to have nothing. In 1 Corinthians 13, Paul says it better than anyone else:

> If I speak in the tongues of men and of angels, but have not love, I am only a resounding gong or a clanging cymbal. If I have the gift of prophecy and can fathom all mysteries and all knowledge, and if I have a faith that can move mountains, but have not love, I am nothing. If I give all I possess to the poor and surrender my body to the flames, but have not love, I gain nothing. . . . And now these three remain: faith, hope and love. But the greatest of these is love (1 Cor. 13:1-3, 13, NIV).

In my book, *Dad the Family Counselor*, I deal with the Fatherhood Function "To Love" and give practical coaching tips on how to cultivate a loving heart in your children. The absolute bottom line for equipping children to learn is to demonstrate your love for God and your wife in terms they can understand and to love your children using their own unique love language.

Love is action. Love leads to a servant heart, to otherscenteredness. By that, I do not mean self-neglect, but an orientation toward others. Look after others as you would look after yourself.

A servant heart is my wife's strong suit and my weakest area. Most of what my children learned about a servant heart came from their mother. No one has taught me more about a servant heart than Sandy. Service happens to be her primary love language. The children picked up what they have of a servant heart from watching her through the years.

I present a good case study of the bad effects of not having a servant heart. I am getting better, men. But my kids would be much more advanced had I done better as a younger man.

You can tell how important a servant attitude is to God by the premium He places on it:

Whoever wishes to become great among you shall be your servant, and whoever wishes to be first among you shall be your slave; just as the Son of Man did not come to be served, but to serve, and to give His life a ransom for many (Matt. 20:27-28).

Dr. Howard Hendricks, my old seminary professor and mentor, said, "Develop a servant attitude and the whole world will beat a path to your door."[3] In our society, a servant heart sticks out like an iceberg on the Sahara.

The way to cultivate a servant heart in a child is to model it, demonstrate it, honor it, and reward it. Besides watching Sandy all their lives, our children have been exposed to many other models who have demonstrated a servant attitude.

Roc Bottomly attended Dallas Seminary with me and came to work at Kings Arrow Ranch for one summer. For some reason, I had erroneously associated a servant heart with the female gender role, but Roc showed me that real men thrive on serving others. He seemed preoccupied with scanning the horizon looking for places to serve.

At the ranch house, he leaped to carry everyone's dishes to the kitchen. He considered it his private privilege to sponge off the table after every meal. He constantly waited on his wife, Bev, and the kids. He always volunteered to do the dirty work around the ranch in his free time. When his camp counselors drew KP, trash run, or bathroom detail, Roc led the way.

His example made me reconsider my bias against a servant attitude. For the first time, I began thinking of serving others. Roc helped train me.

Another example of a servant heart in action occurred at our family ski vacation during Christmas in a beautiful condo at Vail, Colorado, as the guests of Chuck and Carol Meyer. Living intimately for a week with Chuck gave me new insight into the servant skills of a family shepherd.

Chuck spent each day serving his family, our family, and the Skip and Michelle Coffman family. He braved the mountain weather to do all the grocery shopping. He arose early each morning and cooked breakfast for all. An expert double black diamond skier himself, he forsook his level of skiing and dedicated every hour on the ski slopes supplying the rest of us with ski lessons. He drove everyone around in his Jeep. Chuck's most frequent statement was, "It doesn't matter to me. I'll do whatever you all want to do."

I figured if Chuck can serve without jeopardizing his masculinity, so can I. Chuck helped train me. What can train me can also train you. What can train us can train our children.

I know of a whole community of people who relish playing a servant role. Our family has developed an incredible love relationship with some Cajun families who live in Bayou Lafourche, South Louisiana, below New Orleans. We trek down to "Sportsman's Paradise" about once a year for a visit and a chance to catch boatfuls of speckled trout and red fish. The Reed Danos family, the Hank Danos family, the Charlie Bruce family, and the Lynn Pierce family demonstrate love and a servant attitude better than any others I have known. They are professional servants.

We roll in at any time of the day or night and immediately get slapped with special Cajun cooking. Crayfish, crabs, blackened red fish, Sheila's barbecued shrimp, Charlie's fish soup, and all kinds of casseroles haunt us during the whole visit. They take us out in boats, bait our hooks, and make sure we catch fish. Sandy and Helen caught over 100 speckled trout in less than one hour on our last trip. We have to get rude and pushy just to pitch in and help fillet the fish.

Whenever we return from our Cajun connection, we talk about what great hearts and super servants they are and how much they honor Christ. They always motivate us to get busy and improve our servant style. Many times throughout the year, I remind our kids of the Bayou Lafourche style of servanthood.

LONG-RANGE AIM

Training children is the most difficult task I know. They are always changing; they are hard to understand; and, if things don't work out, you can't fire them or recommend them for early retirement. You are stuck with them, and you must live with all your mistakes. But you also get to live with all the rewards. My only hope has been that God made children the most durable and resilient of all His creatures.

As you work with your children, remember to keep your own act together and concentrate on the tools you need to transfer the inner qualities you wish to impart. Don't worry about temporary setbacks and short-range problems — focus on the long range. You may have to go to a lot of trouble and take risks, but it's worth it.

E-TEAM HUDDLE GUIDE
CHAPTER THREE: DAD THE FAMILY GUIDE

E-TEAM REVIEW
10–15 minutes

Dad, the Family Shepherd

After coffee and fellowship, take 10–15 minutes to allow the men to tell about the results of last week's project. This is the accountability part. Be firm with each other and encourage everyone to complete the projects. If anyone encountered difficulty or had a family problem arise, pause to allow the E-Team to address the problem and pray.

E-TEAM DISCUSSION
50–60 minutes

This part allows you to discuss the key concepts in this chapter and relate them to your individual lives. Be sure to leave time to complete the Workout and Encouragement sections.

THE PRINCIPLES (Check the text for help.)
1. Have an E-Teammate read the list of pneuma, power, and hand tools. Why is a list like this helpful for a father? Comment on this list.
2. Discuss the difference between a person who lives under extrinsic determinism and one who lives under intrinsic determinism.

THE IMPLICATIONS (Why are these ideas significant?)
3. What would a family be like if all the members operated with extrinsic determinism? What would a society be like if the citizens operated with extrinsic determinism? Think of someone you know who operates with intrinsic determinism and describe this person to the E-Team.
4. How can a person switch from extrinsic determinism to intrinsic determinism? How can a person help another make the switch? Why would a person resist help to make the switch?
5. (Extra credit theological question for A students: Is the Old Testament with its emphasis on the LAW an extrinsic system while the New Testament with its emphasis on GRACE an intrinsic system? Be careful: this just might be a trick question!)

THE APPLICATION (How do these ideas affect me?)

6. Briefly describe your family of origin in terms of these two systems.

7. Tell the E-Team about an example or situation in your own life where you labored under extrinsic determinism.

8. Locate each of your children on the scale below by writing their initials on it. Do you think they are at the appropriate level for their ages?

| Extrinsic | | | | | | | | | | Intrinsic |
| Determinism | | | | | | | | | | Determinism |

| -5 | -4 | -3 | -2 | -1 | 0 | +1 | +2 | +3 | +4 | +5 |

E-TEAM WORKOUT
10–15 minutes

Allow each man to choose one of the project options (plays) to perform during the week. If so desired, design your own project. Note: It is essential that each man leave having made a definite commitment to a specific project.

1st PLAY:
Make an appointment with your wife and explain extrinsic and intrinsic determinism. Then show her where you located each child and get her opinion on it.

2nd PLAY:
Make an appointment with your wife and explain extrinsic and intrinsic determinism. Then ask her to describe her family of origin in terms of these two systems. Next, discuss where you think both of you are at this point in your lives.

E-TEAM ENCOURAGEMENT
5–10 minutes

Close the meeting in prayer for each other and your families. Include in your prayer a specific request for spiritual power to successfully complete your project.

BREAK THE HUDDLE, GO HOME AND RUN THE PLAY!

Chapter Four
Dad the Family Trainer

TEACH		TRAIN		TRACK		TEND	
1	2	1	2	1	2	1	2

*"Treat your children as though you won't have
them next year.
Train your children as though they won't have you
next year."*

—*Sandy Simmons*[1]

THE INTERCEPTION

Brandon threw an interception late in the fourth quarter that lost the game for the Robinson Senators. But what Brandon did on the first play of the next offensive series made him a champ in my heart for all time. It wasn't so much the next pass that meant so much to me; it was the thing he did with his mind that made me proud.

It started when he first went out for football in the seventh grade. He came home from his first practice and gave me the grim news that the coach had put him at quarterback. I hate quarterbacks. I love to sack 'em. Sometimes, I get up early in the morning and feel the urge to go in while Brandon's still asleep and pick him up and throw him to the turf.

Anyway, I perceived my duty and commenced to teach him the secret key of success for a quarterback—*Recovery.* A quarterback must recover. He must recover instantly after a mistake. He must remain cool, keep his poise, display confidence, and inspire his team to follow him with vigor after a setback in order to keep mighty momentum from shifting to the opponent.

I began a training routine for Brandon to equip him to recover. This training sequence can be used to train a child to apply almost any principle of wisdom to his behavior. The sequence consists of six parts which I will explain using this football incident.

1. Create the need.
2. Teach the Scripture.
3. Explain the application.
4. Create a slogan.
5. Reinforce the principle.
6. Celebrate the victory.

Create the Need

Brandon, a quarterback, more than anyone else, must completely shake off the last play and start a new game with the next. If he fumbles, misses a coverage read, or throws an interception, he can't let it bother him past the whistle. He must *recover* and come out fighting in the next play. A quarterback must feel no guilt for past errors. He must start every play with supreme confidence and optimistic expectations. He needs to learn the principles of recovery.

Teach the Scripture

I turned to Philippians 3:13-14 and read to Brandon Paul's advice to the men at Philippi on how to recover from mistakes:

> Brethren, I do not regard myself as having laid hold of it yet; but one thing I do: forgetting what lies behind and reaching forward to what lies ahead, I press on toward the goal for the prize of the upward call of God in Christ Jesus.

Explain the Application

"Brandon," I said, "this is how you take Paul's principle of recovery and apply it to football. Son, football is not a sport with sixty plays per game; it is a sport with sixty games per contest. Each play is an entire game in itself. Each play experiences its own lifetime: it gets born (the snap) and it dies (the whistle). Each play contains a goal, a strategy, and twenty-two men exploding with savage violence and frenzied motion for less than ten seconds to attain the wreath of victory or the shame of the vanquished.

"You win or lose each play. Whether you win or lose a play, you approach the next play (game) the same way. Everyone gets up, goes home to the huddle, and decides on another game. When they break the huddle and approach each other for another battle in the long campaign, they all start from scratch again. Each man must forget the last game and focus totally on the next game. As they hunker down at the scrimmage line, all the pieces are set up for another game that each team has a chance to win or lose."

Create a Slogan

I reduced the principle of recovery to a short slogan, "Every play is a new game," and started hammering Brandon with it. Every morning as he left for school, I drilled him: "Remember in practice this afternoon, Son, every play is a new game." When he had tests on school subjects, I pumped him: "Remember, Son, each question is a new game." Before every game, my last words to him were, "What do you need to remember, Son?" Brandon always grinned and replied, "Every play is a new game, Dad. Thanks, Dad."

Reinforce the Principle

Brandon entered high school and started thirty-two games for the Senators. I joined the booster club and worked on the chain gang that handled the first down markers during the home games. I saw lots of close up action as I filed up and down the sidelines and, best of all, I was close enough so Brandon could hear me offering encouragement and coaching tips during the game. Once in a while, we had to trot out to measure for a first down and Brandon and I could exchange pleasantries like, well, "Remember, Son, every play is a new game."

Eventually, Brandon got tested on the principle of recovery. During his fourth game as a junior, the Senators were locked into a grim struggle with a chief rival, J.A. Fair High School. The game seesawed back and forth and late in the fourth quarter, they had the lead and we needed a touchdown to win. The Senators took over on their own 20 yard line and Brandon had to lead them 80 yards in about six minutes to win the game.

Robinson came out of the huddle and lined up on the ball. A light rain had been falling and wetness glistened on the turf. Brandon called the signals and the center snapped the wet football. Brandon had called a play action quick pass to the tight end on a middle slant. As he grappled with the slippery ball, he lost a fraction of a second. He rode the fullback into the two hole a little too far and lost another split second.

By the time he stepped back to fire the pass, the strong safety had read the play and stepped up just after Brandon let fly. He intercepted the pass, dashed through the traffic, and broke out laterally, coming to the side line right toward me. Oh, how I wanted to jump out and tackle him.

Brandon darted over to cover the pass and had the angle on the safety when one of the Fair linemen blocked him out and the runner cut inside and bolted for the score.

In stunned disbelief, I searched the gridiron praying for a yellow flag that would nullify the play. No flag. Six points.

I glanced at Brandon, who lay spread eagled on the 15 yard line not more than ten feet from me. He had his face mask pressed into the sod and was crying and pounding the turf with his fist.

My heart seared with pain. That was my boy out there and he was hurting. I was torn between calling out to him and praying for him. I sort of compromised and called out to him in prayer. I cried out in my mind, "Brandon, Son, let it hurt. Taste the pain. Feel the awesome anguish of failure. Go ahead and get your fill of it. . . . Now, Son, get up. Get up! Get off the field and get yourself ready to play football. Remember, every play is a new game."

Brandon slowly got up and eased off the field. The Fair Falcons kicked the extra point, and jubilantly lined up for the kickoff. We now needed two touchdowns to win the game. We took the kickoff at the 20 and raced up to the 35 yard line. I looked over at our bench and saw Brandon buckle on his helmet and trot out to the huddle.

Robinson broke the huddle, lined up, and snapped the ball. Brandon took the snap, rode the fullback into the two hole and stepped back, raised up, and fired the football to the tight end on a quick slant across the middle. He caught it and gained about a dozen yards and a first down. Brandon marched the team right down the field and moved the ball inside Fair's 20 yard line before the clock ran out.

Do you know how much guts it takes for a quarterback to throw a pass right after an interception? Well, Brandon had pounded his grief over the interception into the field, gone over to the bench, and started repeating, "Every play is a new game. Every play is a new game." He then stepped into the huddle and called the same pass play and rifled a strike to the tight end. Brandon had recovered. He *recovered*. He had been trained to recover and when the pressure hit, he recovered.

Celebrate the Victory

As Brandon walked off the field, I stood waiting for him on the sideline. His eyes were downcast and he carried the weight of the loss on his shoulders. About twenty feet away, he looked up and saw me. He burst into tears and walked up to me, put both arms around me and cried, "Dad, I'm so sorry. I really tried. I did the best I could."

I hugged him back and said, "Brandon, I know it hurts but I want you to know that I have never been prouder of you in my life. I saw the guts of a man out there tonight. You are a champion in my book. I can't imagine the strength and force of will that it took to shake off the interception and come right back and throw the same pass on the very next play. You recovered and it takes a real man to recover like that."

I celebrated his victory of recovery in the midst of defeat. We walked off the field arm in arm in front of all the other players and the staring fans and we were both choking back the tears. I walked into the locker room with him, cut off his ankle tapes and helped him with his shoulder pads, all the while telling him how proud I was of his ability to recover.

I know it's only a game. I know football is kinda stupid. But there was more happening out there that night than a bunch of boys doing what boys foolishly do. There was a young man implementing an important life principle that he learned from his dad.

Sandy and I loitered around the locker room entrance after the game waiting for Brandon to finish his shower and come out. He finally appeared and walked toward us. I braced myself to offer comfort and encouragement. He passed us with a friendly nod and walked over to his pickup truck and started joking around with his friends.

I looked at Sandy and said, "Can you believe that? That boy just lost a football game and look at him. He's over there yucking it up with his buddies. Doesn't he care? Where's his heart?"

Sandy smiled and said, "Maybe he has recovered." And so he had.

I have just described a story about a family shepherd training his son in an important lesson on life using a common sense training sequence. Training children is difficult and time consuming. It drains incredible energy from a father. That's probably why it stands as one of the most often neglected components of the equipping process. It's hard work.

Teaching is not enough. Imparting mere knowledge into a child's skull does not, by itself, build character or change behavior. A process is needed to help the child internalize teachings (to make the knowledge their own) and to develop a responsive system for allowing the wisdom to initiate and modify actual behavior. It takes training to convert knowledge into profitable behavior.

In the last chapter, I covered the prelims of training. This chapter covers the training process and gives coaching tips and case studies on how to apply these training principles.

THE TRAINING STAGES

From birth to maturity is from here to eternity.

In my mind, the one word that associates with *child* is *change*. Children constantly metamorphose. Even Jesus went through a maturing process: "And Jesus grew in wisdom and stature, and in favor with God and men" (Luke 2:52, NIV).

Jesus matured through levels of intellectual, physical, social, and spiritual development. Paul passed through a milestone as well as he passed from childhood to manhood. "When I was a child, I talked like a child, I thought like a child, I reasoned like a child. When I became a man, I put childish ways behind me"(1 Cor. 13:11, NIV).

Even King David had a father-son talk with his son Solomon about manhood. " 'I am about to go the way of all the earth,' he said. 'So be strong, show yourself a man' " (1 Kings 2:2, NIV).

Fathers who study the child developmental stages have an incredible advantage over those who have little insight as to where their children are in the process. They can anticipate and prepare properly to help the children go through each phase. They know what is appropriate and normal behavior in each phase and understand that no phase is permanent. Not knowing these stages can lead to two major fatherhood errors:

1. *Underestimating your child*, which retards normal development. The child does not receive the proper stimulation and prompting that causes growth and strength.

2. *Overestimating your child*, which overwhelms the child. The child spends his childhood constantly trying to catch up with what's expected of him or her only to finally arrive and find the standards pulled higher, just out of reach again. This causes children to develop a shame base and a deep pain pool.

Louise Bates Ames, cofounder of Gesell Institute of Human Development, writes:

> The most common mistake parents make is not understanding what
> children are like at different stages of development and therefore ex-
> pecting too much. Fathers often do this more than mothers. They say:
> "It's time that he was toilet-trained," or "it's time that he fed himself."[2]

There's no need to get upset when the toddler knocks over a glass of milk. They specialize in overturning liquids. That's what little kids do for a living. You might as well figure that your child has been assigned to waste a quota of 1 million squirts of frothy milk from some poor ole hard-working Holstein cow. Just patiently keep tabs of the total until he reaches his quota, then he can stop batting glasses around.

From birth to maturity is an odyssey of massive magnitude equivalent to a voyage by the *U.S.S. Enterprise* on *Star Trek*. On the bridge of this great starship there are thousands of dials and gauges that measure everything from warp speed to galaxy position. The long voyage from birth to maturity contains many positions, speeds, and milestones that can be defined and logged to make fathering a more predictable journey. After much study of the experts, I find it helpful to designate ten separate developmental phases, or positions, a child moves through by age eighteen (see Figure 17).

Flowing through these ten stages are four primary indicators, or gauges, that measure the level of the child's development as it pertains to methods of training and discipline. These four gauges are the mental gauge, the moral gauge, the behavior gauge, and the cooperation gauge (see Figure 18). These gauges measure the level of the child's ability to respond to training and discipline as he or she progresses in the maturing process. By studying a child and checking these gauges, a father can tell what a child's capabilities are.

Space does not allow a complete explanation of each of these categories in the text, but I have included it in Appendix H. Please consult the appendix to check the characteristics of the age bracket of your children. This will give you a great advantage in understanding your child and matching proper training techniques.

The gauges move from irresponsibility to responsibility and from a level requiring extrinsic controls to one where intrinsic control is

THE TEN DEVELOPMENTAL PHASES OF CHILDHOOD									
1	2	3	4	5	6	7	8	9	10
THE UNBORN PHASE	THE CREEPER PHASE	THE TODDLER PHASE	THE DYNAMO PHASE	THE SOCIAL PHASE	THE BUDDY PHASE	THE MODELER PHASE	THE PUBERTY PHASE	THE ADOLESCENCE PHASE	THE QUEST PHASE

In Appendix G, I have presented a scouting report on each of these phases. You may want to look up the phase your children are in and note what you can expect from them.

Figure 17

in place. Meanwhile, the three levels of maturity development require different correctional techniques that will be developed throughout the rest of this book, especially chapters 7 and 8.

This chart is not as cut-and-dried as it appears. Movement through the levels rarely happens smoothly or on time. Each child goes through it at a different pace. There is no clean break when the child moves into a new level. Children start, stop, regress, leap forward, stall, and spin through these levels. Also, a child can be at different levels in different categories at the same time. For instance, a boy may be thinking conceptually but tied down in total dependence, or a girl could be controlling her behavior by perceptions but trapped in self-focus judgment.

Notice also that each level demands a different fathering approach. Your role begins as a trainer who gets on the field and walks the child through the plays. Later you function like a coach who calls the plays and encourages the child from the sideline. Finally, you move up into the stands and become the greatest fan in the stadium, but you stay off the field during the game.

THE FOUR MATURITY GAUGES

> —————————— MATURITY ——————————————▶

IRRESPONSIBLE —————————————	RESPONSIBLE
EXTRINSIC _____	INTRINSIC
CONTROL	CONTROL

Category	LEVEL I	LEVEL II	LEVEL III
MENTAL	Concrete Thinker	Logical Thinker	Conceptual Thinker
MORAL	Self-Focus Judgment	Others-Focus Judgment	Principle-Focus Judgment
BEHAVIOR	Control by Instincts	Control by Modification	Control by Perceptions
COOPERATION	Total Dependence	Careful Independence	Healthy Inter-dependence
FATHERHOOD ROLE	Trainer	Coach	Fan

(For a full explanation of these categories, see Appendix H.)

Figure 18

The philosophy behind this approach is to start out with extrinsic motivation and move to intrinsic motivation as fast as you can but as slow as you have to considering the four natural gauges. Thus, a fundamental principle in good fathering is: There is no substitute for intensely observing your own unique child and drawing your own conclusions. This chart and the following comments will help you in your evaluation process.

THE TRAINING TECHNIQUES

Since the following coaching tips make sense to me, I try to follow them as closely as possible. But, as you study them, remember that the real difficulty here is application, because your family and situation are unique. At some point, you must weigh what I write, analyze your family situation, discuss it with a few trusted friends, and make the decision on how to handle things.

Child training is a contract between the parent and the child about what is expected. There is no contract without a meeting of the minds. Training begins with a clear assignment. No child can be happy unless he or she knows what he or she is supposed to do, how to do it, and how well it must be done. A good assignment contains four elements:

1. The Goal—what behavior, activity, or goal is expected.
2. The Limits—the scope, boundaries, or limitations.
3. The Procedures—the steps and sequence of activities.
4. The Quality—the level of acceptable performance.

This section deals with how to make a good assignment, while chapters 5–8 cover how to follow up the assignment, track, and tend.

The Clear Father

The goal in giving an assignment is understanding—not necessarily agreement, but a comprehension of the goals, parameters, standards, or behaviors. For instance, your child may not agree that 11 o'clock is a delightful curfew, but there should be no confusion that the child will be home when the clock strikes 11.

The responsibility for clarification lies with you. Don't assume: Assumptions make fools of us all. Put it in writing, ask the child to repeat it, do whatever it takes to prove that all parties clearly understand what is expected and what the consequences are. Explanations should always be in the terms the child understands.

My goal for Brandon was not to be a great quarterback. Football served only as a medium, a practice field. My goal centered on equipping Brandon to deal with mistakes and disappointments in life. My goal was to teach him how to recover from adversity. I merely used football as a medium because he had a strong desire to excel in football, and I had established credibility in the field.

I took great pains to explain the biblical principle of recovery to

Brandon. I read Philippians 3:13-14 and discussed it at length. Then I related the principle to football and put it into the form of a slogan: "Every play is a new game." This helped get the concept into his mind in a practical, usable form that had value to him.

The Realistic Father

All goals and behaviors must be realistic, reasonable, and attainable. Keep the child's personality and developmental phase in mind. A child in Level I thinks in concrete terms, so be specific and don't expect a long retention span. If you tell the infant "no, no" as he or she reaches for a figurine, don't expect him or her to remember it a week later. This would not be disobedience, it would only be instinctive curiosity. In this case, you should childproof your house.

At Level II, don't expect a child to retain a long sequence of ideas or instructions. To a thirteen-year-old boy, long-range planning amounts to about three hours and what they can snack on after dinner. At Level III, allow room for personal preference, prudence, and discretion. When I was an upperclassman in high school, my dad tried to plan my dates for me. He told me where to go, what to do, and when. One of the most shaming things Dad did was demand I be home at 10 o'clock, no matter what. I can remember having to get up in the middle of a movie in front of all the other teenagers and leave my buddies or my date just to satisfy my dad's arbitrary whim.

All consequences and repercussions must be realistic, appropriate, and imbued with justice. The primary function of consequences is to teach a child reality and truth about the principle of cause-and-effect that governs life. The whole idea behind establishing goals and consequences is to teach that "you reap what you sow." This issue of consequences includes some of the most important "heart-ware" your child will ever absorb.

Avoid statements like the following:

"If you break curfew again, you will be grounded for a year!"

"If you talk to me like that again, you will not get any Christmas presents."

"You must make straight A's in school, or you will never amount to anything."

The Reasonable Father

Don't shoot for a perfect kid. No such thing exists. If it did, you, like me, wouldn't deserve one. Don't bother to correct every little thing you see wrong. A child can handle only a certain quota of correction in any given period of time. Too much or too harsh correction can provoke a child to rebellion. Weigh each situation. Will the wrong behavior really matter? Will your child grow out of it naturally? Will natural consequences correct it without you stepping in again? Are there other more important things that need correction?

Helen had a little problem with her room for a while, but she has since overcome it. I worked on her in this way:

"Helen," I said, "they are sending a film crew from Hollywood to make a movie of your room! They are going to call it *Helen's Room Versus Godzilla*, or maybe *Helen's Room Eats New York*. Helen, maybe I can get some wooden pegs and nail them to the floor so your clothes would at least look like they were hung up."

"You really have sick humor, Daddy. Is that the kind of humor you want me to grow up with?" was her reply.

Bless her heart. Helen has many outstanding qualities. She is an outstanding chef, creative designer, shrewd shopper, and excellent home keeper, and she kept her room spotless until she turned sixteen. Then it seemed as if she had abandoned her room to chance. She simply had to have a little patch of turf to keep as messy as she desired. And it sure was!

We told her a million times to clean up her room. We tried everything and failed. The age of correcting her with power had passed. But we kept trying by way of reminder. If it was good enough for the Apostle Peter, it's good enough for Helen.

> Therefore, I shall always be ready to remind you of these things, even though you already know them, and have been established in the truth which is present with you. And I consider it right, as long as I am in this earthly dwelling, to stir you up by way of reminder (2 Peter 1:12-13).

So, if Peter considered repetition a bona fide method of ensuring performance with his adult parishioners, why not utilize it on children? The question arises, if children should be trained to obey the first time, what place does repetition have in retargeting techniques?

The answer lies in the heart of the child. If the child has set his or her will against yours and deliberately disobeys, then you need to apply correction. But children often simply forget, don't notice, or don't remember. They do not have a rebellious will; they merely have immature powers of concentrated focus. They really do forget. They tend to relapse into their natural "bent" and forget their rules and training. Because of Helen's natural "bent" to keep her room "comfortable and livable," we had to issue maps to those passing through her portal.

Helen's case was not rebellion that demanded correction. This was not a test of wills. In this one area, she still floundered in the training stage. She just needed continued training. If we had come down severely on this issue, we would have stripped her gears. Instead, we relaxed and kept in the training mode on this issue far longer than normal but as long as this situation demanded.

Helen now lives in an apartment and keeps it spotless. In fact, she complained over the phone the other day that Brandon (a freshman) brought a bunch of boys over on a Saturday and turned the place inside out, and that it took her two hours to get it back in order.

The Supportive Father
Make sure the child understands the reason for the agreement. Invite challenge and dialogue over the rules as long as it remains inquiry and not defiance. Children must know the why before they can *own* the what. "Why?" is a perfectly legitimate question and shows an attempt to move toward maturity as long as it is a question and not a challenge.

If your purpose is to lead the child to practice intrinsic motivation, you must help the child take ownership of the agreement. The child must be sold on the importance of the idea enough to make it his or her own. If a child's heart doesn't want it, he or she probably won't get it. This is especially true for habit goals. To form or break a habit, it takes not only knowledge and skill training but also a strong desire.

For instance, if you want your daughter to avoid premarital sex, you may decide that she will not be allowed to date until she is sixteen. Allow her to "herd date" — go out with a group of teens but not pair off. To help her gain ownership of this rule, explain the facts in Figure 19 to her.

In a research study of teens from eight evangelical denominations, the Barna Research Group found that by age eighteen, 43 percent of these churched teens had experienced sexual intercourse

DATING AND INTERCOURSE[3]	
If dating starts at age	% who have sex before 18
12 years old	91%
13 years old	56%
14 years old	53%
15 years old	49%
16 years old	20%

Figure 19

and 65 percent had engaged in fondling breasts or genitals and/or sexual intercourse.[4]

Family conferences are a must for clarification and airing out misunderstandings. Bob Ryan, a father in Springdale, Arkansas, scheduled a weekly meeting around the kitchen table as a "safe zone" for each one of his children to ventilate feelings and opinions without fear. Each child had a chance to explain a gripe and a praise without any reaction or retaliation from anyone else. This carried over into the teen years and allowed Bob and his wife to know exactly what was going on with their children. It also opened the door for a lot of meaningful one-on-one sessions.

Illustrative Father

A child must traverse trying terrain to get from a theoretical concept to practical implementation. They need guidance to discern how to negotiate the road from knowing to doing. To help Brandon master the slogan, "Every play is a new game," I tossed it at him as often as possible in a variety of situations. I showed him how to use it in schoolwork, social situations, athletics, work projects, and around the house. After practice, I asked him how it went and whether he thought about the principle. When we watched college and pro games on TV, I pointed out the principle in action.

If there had been a failure or setback in my life at that time, it would have been good to use myself as a living example of recovery. I could have made case studies out of people we knew and characters in stories or movies.

The Practical Father

Make sure children bear the responsibility. Children must realize that life is a sequence of choices. They either can choose to abide by the rules and benefit from the consequences, or they can choose to disobey and reap the penalty. Either way, it is a choice that they must make. If they choose to disobey, they must understand that they are actually choosing a preassigned set of consequences.

For instance, one father explained to his son that he could not borrow the family car if he chose to drink alcohol because of the danger of an accident, the possibility of a DWI, and the exorbitant rise in insurance costs. The boy took the car and got a DWI. The father banned further use of the car and said, "I'm sorry, Son, that you chose to forfeit the use of the car. I wish you could enjoy the advantage of the car in your social life, but this is a decision you made. I hope that you make better choices in the future and avoid penalizing yourself so much."

The Consistent Father

Fathering is like farming: A lot of work sweat lies between the planting and the harvesting. If a farmer doesn't weed and water regularly, his crop gets away from him. A farmer can't plant and forget it; he can't wait until harvesttime to check for weeds. A farmer must be CONSISTENT and steady if nothing else. He also walks by faith; he does his work and knows his reward waits for him in the future.

Be consistent: Say what you mean; mean what you say; and then back up what you say. A child will get a distorted view of reality if you practice inconsistency. When you change or cancel consequences, you teach your child how to manipulate and exploit people and situations. If your instructions and consequences were reasonable and understood, firm enforcement of the consequences will teach your child dependability and responsibility.

Avoid being a strict punitive legalist, however, that holds the child to the letter of the law when there are extenuating circumstances. Sometimes there is good reason why the child stepped out of bounds. Before administering the consequences, be sure to arrange a hearing. Allow the child to explain. Listen to the heart as well as to the facts. Distinguish between confusion and defiance. Take into account variables and factors that clouded or changed the original agreement.

Check to make sure that the child does not get caught between two contradicting orders as when Brandon once told me, "I'm not to leave the house when you are gone, and I'm not to leave my bike out in the rain — I had to decide which rule to break." Fall back, discuss the situation, and reclarify if need be.

The Honest Father
Be completely honest and truthful. If the child requests a new toy and money is an issue, explain that it is not in the budget — avoid saying you don't have any money and then buying yourself a carton of golf balls.

A DAD, A SON, AND THE TRUTH
When Brandon was about nine years old, he got a little lax on telling the complete truth in a couple of situations. Instead of losing my temper, threatening him, and spanking him, I decided to try a more nurturing approach.

I made an appointment to get ice cream with him and have a father-to-son chat. I told him what a great son and friend he was and how rapidly he was becoming a fine young man. We talked about friendship and important qualities that buddies held in common. When we got around to the topic, I explained that, as his father, I would do anything to help him develop manly qualities. I talked about how truthful Sandy always is and how much I respect her for it. I picked several other men in our church and used them as models. We then discussed Ephesians 4:14-15:

> As a result, we are no longer to be children, tossed here and there by waves, and carried about by every wind of doctrine, by the trickery of men, by craftiness in deceitful scheming; but speaking the truth in love, we are to grow up in all aspects into Him, who is the head, even Christ.

I explained that almost all children struggle with developing truthfulness, but one of the signs of manhood was being a man of truth. Men who enjoy a relationship characterized by truthfulness keep on growing in Christ.

I said, "Son, I would like it if you and I developed a special manly relationship based on truthfulness. Why don't we brainstorm on some ways you could improve in this area and grow into the kind of man you want to be."

We finally came up with a project together. He would take four chapters in the Book of Proverbs, then locate and write down every verse that talked about telling the truth. He accepted the challenge and went to work.

A week later he showed up with pages of verses written out. I couldn't believe it. He had taken the job seriously and completed the assignment. He had taken ownership of this task and adopted the goal. Truthfulness became an inner conviction for Brandon. We never had to worry about him telling the truth again. I have not heard Brandon tell a lie since then. And today, we enjoy an incredible relationship where we are honest and truthful with each other and help each other grow in Christ.

Epilogue

It's late at night in my home, and I just finished writing the paragraph above. Brandon is home for Christmas from his senior year at University of Arkansas. I decided to go in and tell him that I was putting this little story in this book.

I walked into his room and said, "Brandon, I'm in there working on the book and thought I'd tell about the time when you looked up all the proverbs about telling the truth. Do you remember that?"

"I sure do, Dad. You made me look up verses on love, honesty, and wisdom too!"

I felt moved to tell Brandon something special: "Well, Son, I just want you to know that you have developed into the kind of man with the finest inner qualities that I could ever imagine. I feel like I could trust you with anything. If I were looking for a steadfast loyal male friend, you would be my first choice. I just want to thank you for your integrity, Son."

"Dad, I want to thank you. Ever since I can remember, you have conveyed to me that I was dependable. I guess I just grew up convinced that you were right and have tried to live up to that vision of myself that I got from you."

That says it all, folks.

Correct your son, and he will give you comfort;
He will also delight your soul (Prov. 29:17).

E-TEAM HUDDLE GUIDE
CHAPTER FOUR: DAD THE FAMILY TRAINER

Dad, the Family Shepherd
E-TEAM

E-TEAM REVIEW
10–15 minutes

After coffee and fellowship, take 10–15 minutes to allow the men to tell about the results of last week's project. This is the accountability part. Be firm with each other and encourage everyone to complete the projects. If anyone encountered difficulty or had a family problem arise, pause to allow the E-Team to address the problem and pray.

E-TEAM DISCUSSION
50–60 minutes

This part allows you to discuss the key concepts in this chapter and relate them to your individual lives. Be sure to leave time to complete the Workout and Encouragement sections.

THE PRINCIPLES (Check the text for help.)
1. What two common errors do fathers make when they do not understand the developmental stages of children?
2. What are the four elements that make a good assignment?
3. Why is clarification essential when explaining behavior standards to a child?

THE IMPLICATIONS (Why are these ideas significant?)
4. Describe what it must be like for a child when the rules are vague, confusing, and subject to change without notice.
5. What happens in a child's heart when you demand behavior and performance above his or her ability? Below his or her ability?

THE APPLICATION (How do these ideas affect me?)
6. Tell the E-Team what level of development your oldest child is in and what characteristics you have seen that help you determine this.
7. If your children were asked about how clear and precise your family rules and behavior standards are, what would they say?

E-TEAM WORKOUT
10–15 minutes

Allow each man to choose one of the project options (plays) to perform during the week. If so desired, design your own project. Note: It is essential that each man leave having made a definite commitment to a specific project.

1st PLAY:
Train your child to convert a biblical truth into a behavior pattern by choosing a verse, making a slogan out of it, selecting a way to illustrate it, and helping the child practice it.

2nd PLAY:
Make an appointment with your wife and discuss the developmental levels of each of your children.

E-TEAM ENCOURAGEMENT
5–10 minutes

Close the meeting in prayer for each other and your families. Include in your prayer a specific request for spiritual power to successfully complete your project.

BREAK THE HUDDLE, GO HOME AND RUN THE PLAY!

The Fatherhood Function: To Track

Chapter Five
Dad the Family Scout

TEACH		TRAIN		TRACK		TEND	
1	2	1	2	1	2	1	2

"The results of faithful fatherhood far outweigh
any career climb, any economic windfall,
or any position of power and fame that
can be imagined."
—Howard Hendricks[1]

HERE'S EGG ON YOUR FACE
and down your neck

As director of Kings Arrow Ranch, I had to raise donations to finance new construction projects. I planned a fund-raising trip to Mobile, Alabama, and decided to take four-year-old Helen with me on the two-day trip. We got up early, gulped down a hearty breakfast of scrambled eggs, and left for Mobile.

Later, Helen and I sat in the plush waiting room of a large international company, waiting for an appointment with the president. I sat on an expensive designer sofa across from the president's secretary while little Helen stood on the sofa leaning against me. Since she murmured that her tummy didn't feel too good, I got her a 7-Up.

After she drank most of the 7-Up, Helen leaned over to whisper something in my ear just as the president opened his door and the secretary stood to tell me he could see me. As if the president's door had pulled the trigger, Helen threw up. She showered my ear, neck, and suit coat with a tasty mixture of scrambled eggs, milk, and 7-Up. It splashed over the sofa and cascaded down to the expensive carpet.

After I wiped it off my face, clothes, briefcase, and sofa, I scraped it into tidy little puddles on the carpet. Helen sat on the sofa in shifting shades of green. The president and secretary stood gasping in disbelief. Soon, they joined me in blotting up the lumpy yellow porridge with towels. We made our introductions as we worked together there on our hands and knees.

Later, I sat in his office swathed in a thin drying film of egg vomit that had taken on the acrid aroma of hydrogen sulfide. After I gave my presentation, he made a large donation. I believe we became instant friends because our mutual experience of wallowing in Helen's oral discharge had broken down all kinds of barriers. Since then, I have always tried to take sick babies with me to raise donations.

The question: How should I have disciplined Helen?

The answer: No discipline was called for. She only did what little four-year-olds frequently do after a long trip in a car on a full stomach. This was a gastronomical problem, not a behavior problem. When we returned to our car, I hugged her, loved her, and continually told her not to worry about it. If I had blown up, called her names, told her she was stupid, or spanked her, I could have easily done some deep damage. I would have filled up her pain pool and built into her shame base.

Confused Fatherhood

Youth is a wonderful thing: What a crime to waste it on children. Childhood is that magical time when all you need to do to lose weight is bathe. Children are a lower animal form that stands halfway between an adult and the TV. Children are young enough to know everything and give everyone else the full benefit of their inexperience. Children are the Rubik's Cube of parenthood.

Confusion reigns in many homes in the area of child discipline. After you have taught and trained children, how do you keep track of them and keep them going in the right direction? What do you do when you catch them doing wrong? What do you do when you catch them doing right? What do you do when you catch them and don't know for sure if it is wrong or right? Take the following case studies as illustrations:

Mrs. Johnson knew that her two-year-old child, Cathy, was in trouble because the girl had been in her room for over a half hour without making any noise. She walked into the bedroom to discover that her creative offspring had dipped into her diaper, procured some of nature's original play-dough, and had proceeded with a little interior decoration. Dazzled with the texture, smell, and color of her potty-dough, she had painted one wall, polished the furniture, and caulked the holes in the lace curtains with it. (Perhaps she expected an NEA grant!) The mother recovered from her initial revulsion and made Cathy play at helping her clean it up. What would you have done? (Ask her to do the den next?)

Cathy made a habit of her little sport because she received special attention and notoriety from it. Her parents refused to disipline her in any way for fear that it would stifle her creativity and inhibit her natural development.

Little five-year-old Tommy ran out of things to do one day, and out of natural curiosity he began investigating his penis. His mother walked in just in time to catch him observing the elasticity and resiliency of his little tool, and she panicked. She jerked the boy into the kitchen, pulled out a butcher knife, held it under his nose, and said, "If I ever catch you playing with yourself again, I'll cut it off!" What would you have done?

Needless to say, as the boy grew to manhood, he experienced serious sexual dysfunction: He could not get an erection, and he never learned to relate to women.

Smart Fatherhood

Yes, raising children can be confusing. Since there are many gray areas and blurred lines that call for hard-judgment decisions, you need some principles to abide by and some faithful friends in your E-Team to help you make the best decisions. No man can be objective about his family, his occupation, or his sin. You need outside input to keep you on track so you can keep your children on track.

The primary principle for tracking your children is to know where your child stands in the childhood developmental stages and to know your child's heart so you will know what behavior to expect and how to respond with appropriate supervision. Men, we must track our children and keep alert as to how we can serve them and best meet their needs. A shepherd fulfills his responsibility. The writer of Proverbs says it in this way:

> Know well the condition of your flocks, and pay attention to your herds; for riches are not forever, nor does a crown endure to all generations (Prov. 27:23-24).

Here is my paraphrase of this passage:

> Keep your eyes open and know well the condition of your children. Concentrate on the needs of each, for they will soon be grown and gone, and you won't have the resources nor the authority to practice fatherhood anymore.

While we wear the badge of fatherhood, the captain's hat, we must make our children a priority and concentrate on their progress. We need to know their condition and pay attention to them so we can do the job while it can be done. One day it will be too late. You won't get a chance to go back and do it over again. Since you get one shot, you had better pay attention to your kids.

This chapter and the next cover the third step of the Equipping Process Chart, Tracking — how to set up an observation system to register and interpret feedback on your children. After you teach and train a child, you need to track the child through the maturity process. This chapter tells you what to focus on and how to keep your vision clear. The next chapter deals with how to sustain proper growth.

FOCUS ON THE HEART

My dad went to my ball games and kept a telescope trained on me to be sure to catch all my mistakes. Since he wanted me to play a perfect game, he cheerfully contributed his negative observations to me after every game. He never mentioned my good plays. Why should he? They were not the ones that needed to be corrected. My bad plays needed forceful focus to impress upon me the urgency of purging them.

Funny how that always demotivated me. Odd how I tended to make more mistakes as the heat increased. Peculiar how I felt like a failure no matter how successful I really was. Puzzling how I hated to see Dad after any game or task I ever attempted.

Who wants a failure ledger as a legacy? Perhaps Dad should have awarded me turkey trophies and blunder ribbons with which to festoon my hall of shame. No one wanted to succeed more than I did. No one tried harder than I. No one regretted my mistakes more than I.

You track your children to chart their progress, not to record their inadequacies. You want to be person-oriented, not problem/mistake-oriented. Take the attitude that your task is to help them achieve successive levels of maturity, not to eliminate every mistake and flush all problems. If you focus on the person and what he or she is doing right, the problems and mistakes will take care of themselves. If you focus on errors, however, your children will grow up with low self-esteem, and shame.

When tracking your children, it's easy to put your eye on the wrong thing. Many parents commit the mistake of not seeing the child as he or she really is. We will study two wrong viewpoints of children: "Gap Focus" and "Violation Focus." We will then study the viewpoint I recommend—"Heart Focus."

Gap Focus

GAP FOCUS

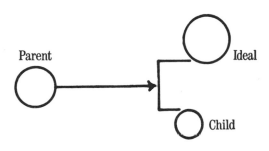

Figure 20

The stage is set for "Gap Focus" when a father imagines the perfect phantom child that he would like his child to become. He then refuses to see his real child. Instead, he concentrates on the differences between his child as he is and the phantom child projected from his own mind. He focuses on the gap between the real child and the phantom child.

In theory, it sounds good. You must have a clear picture of the target if you expect to aim and hit it. A clearly defined goal solves half of any problem. What's wrong with visualizing the goals you have for your children?

The tragedy of "Gap Focus" lies in the viewpoint of children. All they know is that Dad never looks at them. Children spend their childhood having Dad focused over their heads. They never quite measure up to where Dad looks for them. They grow up feeling inadequate with low self-esteem because they feel as though Dad has never accepted them.

Violation Focus

VIOLATION FOCUS

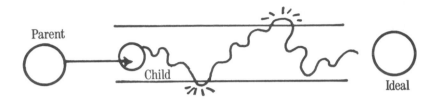

Figure 21

In "Violation Focus" the father creates another perfect phantom child for a target, but this time he doesn't hang it above the child's head for comparison. He correctly projects it way out into the future as an ideal to serve as a guiding star.

He sets up a tracking system with clearly defined parameters of behavior and a precise system of penalties for violations. He provides the child with plenty of maneuvering room and, as long as the child remains within the boundaries of good behavior, the child doesn't incur any penalties.

The father sights his eyes on the parameter lines and stands guard. When the child transgresses the behavior boundary, the alarms ring, the bells toll, the lights flash, and the father comes dashing down the field to the point of violation and administers quick efficient discipline. The father uses "Violation Focus." He focuses on the points of violation.

In theory, it sounds great. He doesn't compare the child to a phantom angel. He establishes everything in advance, and everyone knows the rules and consequences. He acts consistently, impartially, and fairly. Justice reigns.

Look at it, however, from the viewpoint of the child. The child moves through life without careful attention from Dad. Instead, Dad has his eyes locked onto the behavior parameter lines, not the child. The child soon realizes that to get the attention he or she desperately needs from the dominant male caregiver in his or her life, the child must violate a parameter. Then Dad zips in with concentrated attention and intensely interacts with the child.

So what if it's a spanking. That's a good deal. A spanking is a cheap price to pay for special attention from Dad. "Violation Focus" conditions the child to misbehave to get his or her attention needs met. And a child can become an expert at this and hit you when you least want it. Just ask your pastor over for dinner and watch the child go bonkers. Eat out at a nice restaurant with friends and watch your child run amok. A child will do whatever it takes and pay any price to get his or her time with you.

Heart Focus

HEART FOCUS

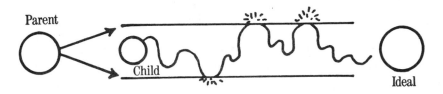

Figure 22

I recommend a tracking system that I call "Heart Focus." With heart focus, you set out the north-star, ideal child, establish behavior parameters, and publish consequences, just as in violation focus. In heart focus, however, you focus on the child's heart instead of sighting down the parameter lines. You do not stalk the child, looking for mistakes. You walk with the child intimately throughout all of his or her acceptable behavior. You get into the child's heart and live with your child.

In the *One Minute Manager*, Kenneth Blanchard and Spencer Johnson write, "The key to training someone to do a new task is, in the beginning, to catch them doing something approximately right until they can eventually learn to do it exactly right."[2] In other words, go home, focus on your child's heart, and catch them attempting to do right; then go bananas with encouragement. Thomas Peters and Robert Waterman, Jr. in *In Search of Excellence* (p. 68), give managers this advice: "Positive reinforcement nudges good things onto the agenda instead of ripping things off the agenda." The best way to keep your children within the behavior boundaries is to constantly focus on the positive things. The more you fill the agenda with positive reinforcement, the more the bad behavior gets nudged away.

When a child approaches a behavior parameter, you are there to gently suggest positive alternatives and nudge the child away from transgressions. If the child persists and violates the behavior code, you still administer correction, but only after you have demonstrated a track record of loving affection and attention. With heart focus, you remove an unhealthy negative compulsion for unacceptable behavior.

I'd like to think that for every one negative correction I make on my children, I have sandwiched it with around seven to ten positive comments.

FOCUS ON AGREEMENT

Childraising is a contractual arrangement. Unless you have a meeting of the minds with your children on what are the precise standards, rules, expectations, and correction policies that exist in your family, you will struggle with confusion and rebellion.

The whole idea is to help a child phase out of dependent extrinsic controls into interdependent intrinsic control. Their ability to establish stable inner control is directly related to the consistency and stableness of the external controls the family provides. Children must know exactly what the rules are in order to eventually write their own "heart-ware" and practice intrinsic motivation.

COACHING TIPS ON
HOW TO ESTABLISH STANDARDS

1. The standards should be clearly defined, recorded, and explained in advance. They should be explained in terms the child can understand and remember. If not, they are invalid. A child can't be held responsible for what he or she can't understand or remember.

2. The standards should be appropriate for the developmental level of the child.

3. The standards should be few, short, and simple to begin with. They can become more sophisticated in time.

4. The standards can vary from child to child. They must be just, but they don't have to be fair. Life is not fair. Each child is unique and needs a set of standards that uniquely fits him or her.

5. The standards should have built-in acceleration and deceleration clauses. If a child gains a new privilege and does well for a while

but then regresses, the privilege should be withdrawn until the child can handle it.

6. The standards should make sense to the child as much as possible. Explain why. The child may not agree, but he or she has a need to understand your reasons.

FOCUS ON THE SPIRIT

As you track your children, special attention must be paid to their spiritual development. You never know what opportunities might suddenly jump up and startle you — like the time when Helen was only three years old and decided to trust Jesus Christ. We were tracking her spiritual development, but this caught us off guard. We thought she was much too young.

I was teaching at a conference over the weekend and Sandy was alone with three-year-old Helen in our home at Kings Arrow Ranch. Sandy stood at the stove cooking dinner while Helen sat playing in her booster chair. It was then that she popped out with these questions about Mrs. Lewis, a dear old lady close to our family who had just died. "Mommy, what happened to Mrs. Lewis? Where did she go?"

Sandy responded, "Helen, wonderful Mrs. Lewis died, and now she is in heaven with Jesus. She is very happy there. We will miss her a lot, but someday, when we go to heaven, we will see her again."

Helen's eyes widened as she contemplated the magnitude of these events, and her little mind began crackling with further questions prompted by Sandy's disclosure. Out came a surprise question: "Mom, what happened to Jesus' mommy?"

Sandy explained that she was in heaven also.

Helen started quietly crying. When Sandy realized it, she walked over, picked her up, and said, "But, Helen, it's not sad because they are both alive and together in heaven right now!"

Helen thought that over carefully and said, "Mommy, I want Jesus in my heart so I can go to heaven too." The thought of Jesus and His mommy in heaven pulled the trigger of her desires, and she wanted to accept Christ right then.

Sandy tried to talk her out of it because she thought a three-year-old couldn't possibly understand enough to make a legitimate decision for Christ. But Helen insisted. After Sandy finally led Helen in prayer, Helen asked Jesus to come into her life and turned her life over to Him.

The next afternoon, I returned home, and Sandy met me at the front door, telling me about Helen's decision. I also thought Helen was too young to know what she was doing. We decided to ask Helen a few basic Campus Crusade, follow-up questions at dinner.

In the middle of dinner, I casually asked Helen, "Helen, Mommy told me that something very important happened yesterday. Do you want to tell me about it?"

"I accepted Jesus into my heart," she replied nonchalantly as she sat in her high chair and continued to eat mashed potatoes, green peas, and roast beef.

I glanced at Sandy for support and asked, "Helen, if you asked Jesus to come into your heart, where is He right now?"

Without an instant of hesitation, she replied, "He's right here!" and pointed to her little chest.

I looked at Sandy, raised my eyebrows, and shrugged my shoulders, indicating that I thought it was a legitimate decision. I didn't know what else to do.

About that time, Helen threw down her spoon, and with her eyes wide with exclamation, she cried out, "Daddy, Mommy, I'm getting food all over Jesus!"

What do you think? Did Helen trust Christ then?

Helen has never questioned whether she became a Christian on that occasion. She looks back to that point as the beginning of her spiritual life. And, we immediately saw spiritual fruit in her life that confirmed her decision.

Helen's decision to trust Christ and start her eternal walk with the Great Teacher did not just happen. It did not occur in a freeze-frame instant of time. She had been in a gradual process of learning over a long period of time. She had heard lots of camp fire stories, camper Bible studies, sermons, testimonies, family devotions, and prayers. She heard our family talk naturally about Jesus as our friend. Guests in our home talked frequently of their ministry through Campus Crusade or their mission field. Bit by bit, Helen had acquired a large pool of teaching on the topic of Jesus and eternal life.

Even though we had been tracking Helen's movement toward spiritual matters for quite some time and had made sure that she had exposure to the truth, we were surprised by her firm desire to trust Jesus Christ. This experience with Helen taught us the importance of tracking your child's spiritual life.

FOCUS ON IDENTITY

Maybe all men are created equal—but all children are created unique. They are like snowflakes: No two are alike. This fact makes fathering all the more difficult because techniques that work on one child will backfire on another. A father must adjust his fathering techniques to match the peculiar "bent" of each child. This means the father must know his children well enough to differentiate their personality types and meet their needs accordingly.

One of my friends has a quiet sensitive son who demonstrates great empathy for people. He likes school and functions as a peacemaker in the youth group. He is obedient, avoids conflict, and promotes teamwork. My friend finds that calm logical reasoning works best for correction and discipline with this boy. He helps him set lots of intermediate goals for big projects and encourages him frequently. He uses a mild voice with him. Sometimes even a command gaze does the trick.

His other son, Conan the Terrible, has a will as strong as Vietnamese horseradish. He demands control and wants things to go his way, which usually results in accomplishing great tasks with people strewn about at the finish line. He is blunt, high-strung, and quick to step on toes. My friend keeps him in control by constantly relating his behavior specifically to his goals. He gets the boy started by pointing at a challenging goal and letting him loose after carefully defining the boundaries. He frequently gets tough with the boy and uses firm voice command.

If my friend treated both boys alike, he would probably ruin both of them. He seems like an entirely different father when he is with one or the other.

My daughter, Helen, is a social butterfly. If she stood in line for a bus, she would organize the other children and get them to elect her president until the bus came. She is off the chart on verbal skills and loves to conceptualize and exaggerate about people, books, and movies. Her idea of a great time is teaching high school seniors English literature. She plays for the crowd and basks in attention. She has been known to cut corners and fudge a little. She knows no strangers. Her emotions gush from her pores. To motivate Helen for a task, all I ever had to do was show her how it would help her make more friends. To get her to do things she doesn't want to do takes firm persuasion.

Brandon, my son, is just the opposite. Mr. Straight will do everything ever required of him with excellence before he is even asked. He always wants to do the "right" thing and has extremely high standards. He micromanages his money and hates debt. He sets high goals and overachieves. He doesn't enjoy conflict. He is a meticulous shopper and an analytical problem-solver. He keeps his emotions to himself and is supercautious in his relationships. For correction and direction, all Brandon needs is to be told and given a little logical explanation.

If I told Helen to "tighten up, get in gear, or else!" I would end up having an "else" stuffed and mounted. I wouldn't think of telling Brandon to do a task because it would win him a lot of friends. I would never use power or force with him. A casual comment and explanation would do for him where Helen would see this as an opening gambit for a discussion or debate. No, Sandy and I have never used the same style of parenting with our children. We have seen the folly of trying to treat them alike. We are fair and firm, but we are radically different with them.

As you track your children, you need to take special pain to discern the personality of each child and to tailor your fathering style to match.

1. Start a dossier on each child. Collect pictures, records, statistics, schoolwork, art work, and personal notes that capture your children's uniqueness, and chronicle their development.

2. Schedule regular family meetings and solicit feedback and personal expression from each child. Record by tape or make notes, and file in the dossier.

3. Schedule personal appointments or activities when you isolate the child and get personal feedback. Ask open-ended questions and probe with "feel" queries. Make records and file.

4. Interview key people involved in special interaction with your children, such as school teachers, church youth workers, coaches, or parents of friends. Make records and file.

5. Take advantage of professional testing and research services to discern learning preferences, personality traits, and aptitude. I highly recommend the DISC Profile from Carlson Learning Company, Family Discovery Network (less than $20 per child), which can be ordered through the Dad the Family Shepherd office (501-221-1102).

6. Study the current youth culture and be aware of peer pressure. Your children are not like a bacteria culture that can be isolated in

---

THE DISC PERSONALITY INVENTORY

The Child Discovery Profile[3] is a self-administering, self-scoring, and self-interpreting instrument designed for children ages four–fourteen. It is based on the concept of four personality types and will reveal the following about each child:

---

1. Degree of people/task orientation
2. Degree of active/passive orientation
3. Greatest strengths
4. Natural limitations that need correction
5. Communication style
6. Social and personal fears and apprehensions
7. How behavior changes under pressure
8. Philosophy of money
9. Decision-making style
10. Greatest needs
11. Recovery preferences

Figure 23

a petri dish and develop without any alien contamination. Never underestimate the power of peers to influence your children. It helps to know about the nature of the youth culture so you can help your kids develop defenses against the most dangerous aspects of it.

You need to pay attention to the music that dominates the youth scene. In the forties, bright hopeful music filled the airwaves. The fifties saw the merging of jazz/blues and upbeat suburban emphasis on sex: Elvis launched rock and roll, and the kids became addicted to dancing. In the late sixties and early seventies, radical political and drug themes took over, and the kids stopped dancing to turn on, tune out, and become spectators at large exhibitionist concerts. The heavy dance beat of the disco days in the late seventies and eighties got the kids up and dancing again. In the nineties, a polarization is taking place. First, there is a romantic and dancing trend. Second, out of the punk and drug culture a sadistic vulgar satanic New Age emphasis with plenty of violence has arisen. The third wave, "Rap," is a cry for help from a group of kids struggling

119

for their own identity and self-expression.

Another area you need to know about is the peculiar set of standards and values that the youth culture abides by. Some groups adhere to extremely structured and strict conduct like gangs, political groups, athletic teams, and school clubs. Others hang together with less formality. One recent study shows there is a significant difference between boys and girls in the criteria for group membership (Figure 24).

CRITERIA FOR CROWD MEMBERSHIP[4]

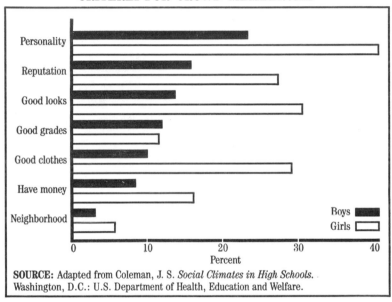

SOURCE: Adapted from Coleman, J. S. *Social Climates in High Schools.* Washington, D.C.: U.S. Department of Health, Education and Welfare.

Figure 24

Your task, Dad the Family Childologist, is to become the world's greatest expert on each child so you can maximize your effectiveness in meeting their special needs as you track them through the maturity process.

FOCUS ON BOUNDARIES

My dad tried to train me to love fighting when I hated conflict. He tried to train me to love baseball when I couldn't hit to save my life. I enjoyed going to home plate next only to getting molar root canals. He conditioned me to like certain athletes and teams and hate others. He tried to train me to display stern, macho behavior, and suppress all hints of sympathy, tenderness, and sensitivity.

Dad violated my personal boundaries. He tried to tinker with facets of my personal being that are off-limits to others. Each child has a cluster of "inalienable rights endowed by our Creator" that are not ethical or moral items but a reflection of the "bent" or spin that God puts into his or her personality. These issues lie outside the scope of the Fatherhood Mission Statement.

It's Dad's business if I cheat in school, bully my friends, neglect my homework, or paw women. It's my business whether I like playing the flute or hitting a blocking sled, like reading history or watching the Gillette Cavalcade of Sports, like blondes or brunettes, enjoy mechanics or carpentry. Some dads have even tried to train a left-handed child to be right-handed.

When a father seeks to train a child to adopt his own discretionary preferences, he abuses the child and wounds his or her soul. The child can't always discern when Dad's goal pertains to ethical behavior or personal penchant and feels guilty or shamed if his or her nature doesn't line up with Dad's demands. The child begins to feel as though his or her personhood is defective.

My friend, Pat Springle, in his book, *Codependency*, describes our inner private zones like ranches on the plains of Texas. We each have a deed to our land and the right to protection from outside interference. In any matters regarding the laws of the state and marketplace, I must comply, but I am free within the boundaries of my ranch to make my own choices as to what crops to raise, what livestock to breed, when to paint the fence, and where to dig the well.

If a man leans over my fence and starts commanding me to plant corn instead of wheat, raise sheep instead of steers, paint my barn, or dig for artifacts, then he is violating my boundaries. If I let him dominate me, I become codependent, and we both lose. I can listen and weigh his advice, but I should be free to make my own choices and face the consequences on the issues within the boundary of my ranch.

When I was younger and didn't know better, my fathering methodology featured a lot of violation focus that infringed on my children's boundaries. I also used a lot of shame-inducing terminology. Don't do it as I did it, men. Benefit from my bungled attempts like the perennial problem of the boy and the garbage.

Brandon has a vision problem. He doesn't see garbage. Something in his eyeball filters out light rays reflected by garbage. One of his duties since age six has been to automatically take out the kitchen trash whenever it needs it. But the trash can rear out of the can and writhe down the hallway into the bedrooms. People can get stuck in it and be falling over it, and Brandon will gaze in blind wide-eyed wonder when we run his hands over it to prove that it's really there.

If I've told him once, I've told him a million times, "Brandon, take out the trash. Son, do I have to tell you every time for the rest of your life? What are you going to do when you have a family — camp out on a deep-burning garbage fill so you will feel at home?"

"Great, Dad. That's really sick humor. Is that the kind of humor you want me to grow up with?"

And then, twice a week, after the garbage truck picks up the garbage, he never never never brings the two big garbage cans back to the house. We spend all our time nearly wrecking our cars trying to run the garbage-can gauntlet down our driveway. I have to tell him every time.

What am I going to do? When he went into high school and reached six feet in height, I discerned that his power lift (spanking) days were over. Again, I just kept on telling him. Repetition. At its worst. Both our nerves were frayed. But the honest truth is that Brandon is an incredible worker, who shows eager initiative and perseverance. He is loyal and generally obedient.

Maybe it is his eyes. For instance, some people can't see colors. Brandon may have a slice of his visual spectrum missing. Or he just forgets. He truly doesn't see it and feels bad when I have to remind him. He repents and asks for forgiveness. He doesn't need severe correction. That's just the little boy still left in him. I need to keep believing in him.

The other day, he drove home from college, parked his car, and got out. As I stood on the porch eagerly waiting to hug him, he ignored me. He turned around, walked off the driveway, and picked up the two garbage cans that I had left out there for two days. I had never noticed them as I careened around them into my driveway. Brandon brought them back and just grinned at me. I know he wanted to say, "Dad, you have a vision problem . . . "

I made a lot of mistakes, men, but I'm glad I didn't make garbage an issue that killed our relationship. I continued to love Brandon and believe in him and kept our relationship healthy.

E-TEAM HUDDLE GUIDE
CHAPTER FIVE: DAD THE FAMILY SCOUT

Dad, the Family Shepherd
E-TEAM

E-TEAM REVIEW
10–15 minutes

After coffee and fellowship, take 10–15 minutes to allow the men to tell about the results of last week's project. This is the accountability part. Be firm with each other and encourage everyone to complete the projects. If anyone encountered difficulty or had a family problem arise, pause to allow the E-Team to address the problem and pray.

E-TEAM DISCUSSION
50–60 minutes

This part allows you to discuss the key concepts in this chapter and relate them to your individual lives. Be sure to leave time to complete the Workout and Encouragement sections.

THE PRINCIPLES (Check the text for help.)
1. Describe the differences between Gap Focus, Violation Focus, and Heart Focus.
2. Why do you need a contractual arrangement with your children on the family and behavioral rules? What are the best ways to make sure you have a meeting of the minds with your children on rules?

THE IMPLICATIONS (Why are these ideas significant?)
3. Do you agree or disagree that a father should treat each child alike? Why or why not?
4. How do you suppose children feel when their personal boundaries are violated? What kind of damage does this do to children?

THE APPLICATION (How do these ideas affect me?)
5. Tell the E-Team how your children differ from each other. If you do not have two or more children, tell how the children in your family of origin differed.
6. Tell the E-Team where each of your children are spiritually. Do you think they are on track for their age?

E-TEAM WORKOUT
10–15 minutes

Allow each man to choose one of the project options (plays) to perform during the week. If so desired, design your own project. Note: It is essential that each man leave having made a definite commitment to a specific project. In addition to one of these two options, I want to challenge you to order the Child Discovery Profile for each of your children.

SPECIAL PLAY:

I strongly encourage you to order the Child Discovery Profile for each of your children. I know of nothing else that will help you gain more understanding and insight for each child. This tool can give you practical usable information that would otherwise take years of meticulous observation to get. Contact Dad the Family Shepherd, P.O. Box 21445, Little Rock, AR 72221. (Price: $10 each.)

1st PLAY:

Make a dossier for each child. To start it, take a sheet of paper and record the following information on it: Name, nickname, birthdate, name of school, favorite sports, favorite school subjects, names of best friends. Also, review the chart in Figure 18 and the material in Appendix H and write a paragraph describing the child's development level in the categories of life.

2nd PLAY:

Every time my children broke a rule or misbehaved, Sandy and I always tried to find out if we were contributing to the problem in some way. Make sure you have clarification of behavior rules with your children by focusing on their understanding of what you expect of them. Do this with this procedure:
1. Wait for a discipline or behavior problem to arise.
2. Ask the child, "What was your understanding of the rule?"
3. Ask, "What was your understanding of the consequences?"
4. Repeat your child's answer back to him.

E-TEAM ENCOURAGEMENT
5–10 minutes

Close the meeting in prayer for each other and your families. Include in your prayer a specific request for spiritual power to successfully complete your project.

BREAK THE HUDDLE, GO HOME AND RUN THE PLAY!

Chapter Six
Dad The Family Sustainer

TEACH		TRAIN		TRACK		TEND	
1	2	1	2	1	2	1	2

*"Researchers, in a 20-year study, found 85% of
children raised by authoritative parents were 'fully
competent' compared to 30% of children raised by
authoritarian parents and 10% of children raised
by permissive parents."*
— *The Institute of Human Development at the
University of California at Berkeley*[1]

THE RAMBUNCTIOUS RAMBOWS

When Helen entered Baylor University, she struggled for a while trying to get herself positioned in the student body. She looked hard for her "niche." She wanted to find her "fit." She needed to develop her support network and get her need for "belongingness" met.

She had trouble because many of the gifts and strengths that had attracted people to her in high school dimmed when held up in contrast to the luster of many of the Baylor students. Baylor featured beautiful coeds draped all over the campus, each with wondrous wardrobes, signature styles, and manicured personalities. Beaming smiles glistened from within burnished automobiles tooling around the Waco campus. The halls of learning also pulsated with high-octane brain kids.

Amidst all this college world a'plenty, Helen could not compete or find her slot at first. But, she is not without great resources, and it didn't take long for her to put her gifts of leadership, organization, motivation, and creativity to work. She started a football team! The RamBows (from Rambo). And she was the middle linebacker, naturally.

She organized the freshmen girls in her dormitory into a powder puff football squad and entered it into the intramural league on the Baylor campus with about sixty other girls' teams. The RamBows dressed out in camouflage T-shirts and pants, and they painted their faces in olive drab camo paint for each game.

The RamBows were awesome. These fearsome freshmen females blasted through their schedule like Rambo through a rice paddy. They intimidated the independent league, sacked the sorority sisters, and battled their way to an undefeated season and a chance to play in the Women's League Championship Game.

Guess who their unbeaten opponents were. Who would you least want to line up against if you were a RamBow? The Women's Graduate Student P.E. majors! I mean, these girls were tough! Some of them even shaved!

Helen had called home with her weekly sportscasts all season. We enjoyed current updates on injuries, workout schedules, and scouting reports. Now, she approached the Big Game with a volley of daily calls. This was it. All the hard work by the RamBows came down to this final game. Helen was really excited.

And why not? She had looked around for a slot on the campus and had finally notched one for herself. Her identity was wrapped up with the RamBows. She was somebody. She loved it when the girls ganged together at the cafeteria and ate their pregame meals in their RamBow outfits. She belonged. She was a RamBow.

Well, Sandy and I talked it over and prayed about it. I then bought a Southwest Airlines ticket to Dallas, rented a car, drove to Waco, pulled up to the football field about an hour before the Big Game, and surprised the daylights out of Helen. She was ecstatic and could not believe I had showed up for the game. She asked me to lead the olive-shaded RamBow squad in their pregame prayer.

The game started and soon got grisly. Both teams played their hearts out. Helen got knocked out of the game twice. The second time I had to lug her off the field. But when she came to, she looked up, saw her daddy, and bolted back out on the field. She wanted to play well for her dad. Alas, the P.E. power prevailed, and the proud but outcalibered RamBows spiraled down in defeat.

That night, I went out to dinner with Helen and some of her teammates. The next day, Helen took me on a tour of the Baylor campus and showed me where all her classes were, where she ate meals, and so on. Helen's behavior on the tour struck me. I'll never forget it. She held my arm the whole time and introduced me to everything that moved. She wanted me to meet all of her teachers. She introduced me to anyone who even looked like someone she knew. And do you know how she introduced me? She said, "This is my dad! He flew in for the game!"

The RamBow episode taught me one of the most significant principles of child raising: Children flourish when you keep track of them, motivate them, and confirm them when they need it. This story is about how Sandy and I perceived a need in Helen and took precious time and money to keep her moving toward the target. Helen needed encouragement and support. It came across in her phone "sport bulletins" and her letters. We know Helen, and we could see what was going on in her life.

Helen certainly did not crash and burn at Baylor. We found her still winging her way toward the target. She just needed a little boost. Helen knew I didn't come to watch the game. She knew I showed up to confirm and encourage her heart. When she took me around and told everyone that I "had flown in for the game," she wasn't trying to tell them I had flown in for the game. She had a much more serious meaning in her message. She actually proclaimed to Baylor that "My dad just reminded me of how significant and important I am by doing whatever it takes to touch my heart, and I don't need to worry about comparing myself and abilities to anyone else on campus." Helen benefited from having an enthusiastic dad who kept track of her heart.

As "head" of the family, you are the "bishop" or "overseer," who keeps the vision of the family and makes sure it continues to fly toward the target. As you track the family and analyze progress, you must act on your findings in one of the following two ways:

1. If your family is headed in the right direction, confirm the members and encourage them to keep moving.

2. If your family has gone off target, you need to make whatever adjustments are required to get it back on track.

A wise family shepherd knows that confirmation beats correction any day. A child would much rather receive a ton of positive confirmation than an ounce of correction. Children constantly need tending, but they do so much better with encouragement than correction. A child (or anyone) can take only so much constructive criticism and then the point of diminishing returns is reached.

It's far better to make frequent checks and confirm progress in a positive way than to check infrequently and be faced with serious corrective measures. As you analyze your child management style, you may want to plan on about a 90/10 ratio of motivation/ correction. Motivation and confirmation are more pleasant for all and always cost less in effort, in emotional wear and tear, and in money. Motivation before the fact feels positive, while correction after the fact feels negative.

Yes, my friend, your children will bolt out of your life and run their race. They will soar over hurdles and crash into pits. They will line up against giants. They will struggle with issues of the heart. Therefore, children need a family shepherd who will "pay attention to his herd" and "know well the condition of his flock." You must keep your eye on your child's heart and know when to and how to step in to motivate and confirm them in their flight toward their destiny.

As you track your children, look for needs to surface that can swing them off course. Then, jump in with strong motivation and confirmation to help reinforce their emerging "heart-ware" and habits. Habits reinforced are more father-friendly than habits that need to be broken and replaced. This chapter deals with the techniques of reinforcing a child's identity with verbal and action confirmation.

This chapter also tells how to confirm your family and encourage them to stay on track. Chapters 7 and 8 tell how to make corrections and adjustments to get back on track.

ENTHUSIASTIC FATHERHOOD

Youth sports — the killing fields of America. My family belongs to an athletic club in Little Rock, where I recently saw a dad perform a hatchet "coaching job" on his two young basketball boys about six and seven years old. I call it terminal coaching. With deadly serious faces expressing pain, the boys stuttered as they went through their drills. Their drills! Insane! This was no game. Not even practice. They did their deadly dance on the court in a bleak attempt to placate an implacable father.

Through clenched teeth, Coach Farce barked out coaching tips like: "Keep your head up in the turn, Jamie! What's the matter with you? You tired? You wanna go home? Keep your feet moving, Joey! You want Jamie to be better than you? You don't want to play. You wanna be a wimp? Get over here, Jamie! You don't deserve to be on the same court with Joey. Sit down until you decide you can hustle. You wanna go home? You sick? What's wrong with you? You wanna be a girl?"

I felt like using an improper motivation technique on him like jerking him up by the neck and giving him a reverse face-lift or a concave nose job, but his dad had probably already beaten me to it. His dad probably cultivated this gnashing style of fathering in the first place.

He was imprinting horrible pain deep into the tiny boys' hearts. Their little pain pools were deluged with big-league hurt. And, I guarantee neither one of them will touch a basketball again from the minute they can get outside Coach Dracula's oppressive jurisdiction.

No, training by negative reinforcement has a sorry track record to commend itself. When a dominant male authority bursting with father power feeds a boy a steady diet of negative gruel for a long time, the boy suffers self-image anorexia and wastes away to bony incompetence. Character assassination never inspires. And this was a case of punitive fatherhood.

Children need a father oozing with enthusiasm. Your fatherhood technique, by itself, does not matter nearly so much as your attitude. A family shepherd must perform with a flair, with style.

> Shepherd the flock of God among you, not under compulsion, but voluntarily, according to the will of God; and not for sordid gain, but with eagerness; nor yet as lording it over those allotted to your charge, but proving to be examples to the flock (1 Peter 5:2-3).

The Eager Father

It's God's will for us to shepherd with desire and eagerness. Your kids need to know that you are thrilled to be their parents. No greater honor exists than to live in this world beaming with the smug knowledge that you are the "chosen one," privileged to parent your children. Your children need to sense this breathless zeal in you. This is power confirmation.

You think I enjoyed watching Brandon go hitless in twenty straight Little League baseball games in the sultry Mississippi heat? You think I savored Helen's four-hour marathon third-grade dance recitals in the stuffy stale overcrowded school auditorium? I would rather endure electric shocks than many of the functions through which parents must suffer.

But I didn't go to watch swinging bats and dancing feet. I went heart hunting. I showed up vigorously scouring fields and stages for my precious hearts that needed confirmation and encouragement.

And when I glimpsed Helen's heart, I went berserk. When I spotted Brandon's heart, I frothed at the mouth. My eagerness to confirm my children sent them a message: "Keep it up, you're doin' great!"

The Exemplary Father

First Peter 5:2-3 sets forth another major principle for child raising: The Law of Paternal Motivation. If you live what you say, your kids will do likewise. Prove to be an example to them.

The Accountable Father

There are two extremes on this emotional issue of family power and control. There is the male chauvinist, who holds that a father exists as an assertive, supreme commander-in-chief of the family. Peter warns against this type of behavior. He cautions not to lord it over those under you. Fathers are not to lord it over their families. But there is also the liberated Mr. Mom, who says the man should be a passive, androgynous, egalitarian type.

Is the family a democracy where the kids can outvote Dad, a monarchy with Dad above the law, or a kind of Christian benevolent dictatorship where everyone trusts Uncle Dad with the reins of power? Who really is in charge of family rules, roles, finances, goals, structure, and child discipline? Who should tell the kids what to do, why it must be done, and what will happen if it doesn't get done? And who says who should? And why should the children obey? Why?

Some fantasy fathers live in a make-believe world, where they perceive themselves as lord, master, king, and sovereign ruler of the family. Dad the Family Tyrant? Surprise! Even the king is not above the law and the Royal Shepherds need to read about the family Magna Carta. The Bible teaches that the father is not the dictator of the home; he is the steward of the home. He himself exists in a chain of command and works under a higher authority—God. This makes the family a theocratic republic and God rules through His document—the Bible.

The word tyrant (from the Greek term *tyrannos*) means a secular ruler who rules without the sanctions of religious law and one whose authority has not been established by religion. Christian men cannot function as tyrants outside the chain of command, apart from the will of God, and lording it over the family members for personal gain.

It's not realistic for a wife and children to slavishly defer and obey every whim of a father who places himself outside the chain of command of God. It is more realistic to expect the family to respect a father whose complete trust is in the Lord and who places himself under His authority. The centurion who approached Jesus in Capernaum won the respect of Jesus because he understood authority and chain of command and explained his power over his troops in terms of his obedience to Rome.

Dad the Family Disciplinarian exercises delegated authority from God to accomplish His will. A father must fit into God's governing structure if he expects his family to fall into formation with him.

CRUCIAL FATHERHOOD

Children need a positive experience with their fathers. A negative father causes damage that not only can ruin the child but also can impact whole nations in a negative way.

The Destructive Father

What do Hitler (fuhrer), Stalin (dictator), Lee Harvey Oswald (assassin), Jesse James (outlaw), Michael Jackson (singer/dancer), and David Rothenberg (burn victim) have in common? They all had fathers who did not provide enough support. Their dads did not make them feel loved and each responded in their own way.

Hitler and Stalin had alcoholic fathers who beat them mercilessly. Oswald's dad abandoned him, and his powerful dominant mother raised him.

Jesse James' father was a preacher from Missouri who began two congregations and helped found William Russell College. During the goldrush, he became very concerned about the spiritual condition of the miners. Because of the difficulty of moving his young family, Rev. James decided to leave them behind and become an itinerant minister in southern California. Shortly after arriving there, however, he became ill and died, leaving his two young sons and a newborn daughter in the care of their mother. The dynamic legacy begun by Rev. James was lost amid the turmoil and later notoriety of his troubled son.

Michael Jackson says, "My father has always been something of a mystery to me and he knows it. One of the few things I regret most is never being able to have a real closeness with him."[2] His strict father beat all of the children with a belt or switch, most of all

Michael, who would fight back. Jackson says, "I'm one of the loneliest people in the world."

David Rothenberg whimpers, "I never want to see my father again. He still wants to be my father, but that can never be." What do you think? His dad poured kerosene around David's bed in a motel room and lighted it. His son suffered third-degree burns over 90 percent of his body and has undergone more than 100 painful skin grafts and other reconstructive surgery.

Killer dads: There are too many destructive fathers in our world today. Children need positive loving fathers.

The Dedicated Father

A father without love is like the sun without light. What good is it? Loveless fathers have done more damage than all the tyrants in history.

Discipline demands love. Love demands discipline. Lack of discipline shows an uncaring callous heart. One teenager, who had been totally neglected by his parents, had wasted his life on drugs, and had been in constant trouble with authorities, once commented, "I wish my dad had said 'No!' just once in my life. Then I would have known he cared."

Parents should discipline their children with the same motive God has in His discipline toward us:

> For whom the Lord loves He reproves, even as a father the son in whom he delights (Prov. 3:12).

> Those whom I love, I reprove and discipline; be zealous therefore, and repent (Rev. 3:19).

Love serves as the basis of all discipline and the motivation for repentance. If you love, you will discipline. If you discipline, you will love. Massive research over the past twenty years shows that these child raising disciplines must not be separated if you want a healthy child.

The Supporting Father

When Art DeMoss died, the Christian world lost one of its great leaders. DeMoss excelled in leadership on an international level because he excelled as a leader in his home. His daughter, Nancy DeMoss, wrote a tribute to him that stressed his life of encouragement. She writes:

I will always think of my father as an encourager and an affirmer. While never tolerating laziness or half-hearted efforts, he encouraged every step in the right direction, thus creating a climate in which we were motivated to do our best. Even in times of failure, insecurity, or inadequacy, he encouraged us to exercise faith in what God could do through the situation. He always sought to encourage us with a vision of what God could do with our lives if they were wholly yielded to Him.[3]

Children desperately need encouragement, affirmation, and direction from a loving father. Research confirms this fact loud and clear. Dennis Guernsey, executive director of Family Ministries, reports on a landmark research project by the University of Minnesota (Weigart, Thomas and Gecs, 1974) that found what kind of parents raise children who have the following four characteristics:

1. High self-worth.
2. The capacity to conform to the authority of others.
3. Tend to follow the religious beliefs of their parents.
4. Tend to identify with the counterculture.

The research team found that the two most powerful factors influencing children were parental control (discipline) and parental support (felt love). By putting support on the x axis and control on the y axis, a matrix forms that divides parents into four types (Figure 25).

A parent with high support (love) and high control (discipline) produces children with the best traits. These parents communicate love and support yet firmly hold the children to well-defined boundaries. They write in positive "heart-ware."

The children with the worst traits had lots of control but little support from authoritarian (authori-tear-ian: they tear the hearts of children) parents. These are the strict harsh parents, who make their children toe the law in rigid obedience and give them little supportive love. These legalistic parents lay down negative "heart-ware" and rely on external controls.

In a set of longitudinal studies conducted by Diana Baumrind at the University of California, three disciplinary styles were identified that produced different behavior traits in children.

"Authoritarian" parents ("Do it because I'm the parent") were more likely to have discontented, withdrawn and distrustful children. "Per-

THE PARENTAL SUPPORT/CONTROL MATRIX[4]

```
                          HIGH
                         CONTROL

                 Q4                    Q1
            AUTHORITARIAN         AUTHORITATIVE
            Lo  Support          Hi  Support
            Hi  Control          Hi  Control
LOW                                                    HIGH
SUPPORT                                                SUPPORT
                 Q3                    Q2
             NEGLECTFUL           PERMISSIVE
            Lo  Support          Hi  Support
            Lo  Control          Lo  Control

                          LOW
                        CONTROL
```

Q1 – Authoritative Parent   high support   high control
Q2 – Permissive Parent   high support   low control
Q3 – Neglectful Parent   low support   low control
Q4 – Authoritarian Parent   low support   high control

The study shows the following results on how the type of parent affected different traits.

Trait	Authoritative	Permissive	Neglectful	Authoritarian
High self-esteem	1	2	4	3
Conformity to authority	1	2	3	4
Acceptance of parental religious beliefs	1	2	3	4
Identity with counter culture	4	3	1	1

Figure 25

missive" parents ("Do whatever you want") had children who were the least self-reliant and curious about the world, and who took the fewest risks. "Authoritative" parents ("Do it for this reason") were more likely to have self-reliant, self-controlled, contented children.

It was found that 85% of children raised by authoritative parents were "fully competent" compared to 30% of children raised by authoritarian parents and 10% of children raised by permissive parents.[5]

Interesting how the Bible addressed this 2,000 years ago:

And, fathers, do not provoke your children to anger; but bring them up in the discipline and instruction of the Lord (Eph. 6:4).

Fathers, don't use a command style that frustrates your children and incites them to rebel automatically against you and your value system, and then spin out of control. Instead, use God's love and wisdom, be personally involved, and use the proper command style to nourish them with biblical principles that discipline and motivate (My paraphrase of Eph. 6:4).

High control seems quite common among evangelical Christians because of their desire to excel in child raising. Beware, however, of overcorrection. It can damage your child.

Another research project shows a direct relationship between parental types and their children's propensity to alcohol and chemical use (see *Dad the Family Counselor,* 141). The more loving the parents, the more apt the child is to abstain from chemicals. The less love the child perceives, the more he or she tends to use inhalants, hallucinogens, crack, and heroin. Children with little control choose marijuana, while strict, high-control legalistic parents produce children who prefer alcohol, cocaine, and sedatives as their drugs of choice.

This research makes sense because parental love builds an honor-based child with a heart full of joy, while strict legalism without love builds a shame-based child with a large pain pool in his or her heart. Shame-based children full of pain will gravitate toward anything that makes the pain stop. Put on discipline, men, but above all, clothe yourselves in love.

Support is the breakfast of champions. To the victor belongs the positive reinforcement. Encouragement breeds winners. A positive attitude must support training.

I'll never forget a conversation I overheard between head coach Bobby Dodd and defensive coordinator Charlie Tate in practice one fall afternoon at Georgia Tech. Coach Tate buddied up to Coach Dodd and said, "Now, Coach, I told you to watch that Simmons kid play the tackle trap. Did you see it? That dog will hunt!" That little offhand remark probably caused me to make second team All-American that year. I thought I was born to play the trap. I prayed for thirty traps a game because Coach Tate said the trap play was not born that could block that Simmons kid. I believed him.

CONFIRMATION FATHERHOOD

Confirmation is in the ear of the beholder. Children need to actually hear confirmation. You need to be verbal with it. Verbal confirmation should take place every single day for all the little things that life is made up of. Here are some examples of verbal confirmation:

"Helen, I thought it was great when you hopped up and helped with the dishes tonight without being asked."

"Brandon, it sure meant a lot to me when you washed your mother's car this afternoon."

"Helen, you did well when you picked up your toys."

"Brandon, you showed a lot of character when you ran your heart out in the mile run even though you knew you couldn't win the decathlon."

"Helen, you can't imagine how much we respect you when you sacrificed your free time to help the girls finish the work in the camp kitchen."

"Brandon, when I saw you drop that bill in the church offering plate, I rejoiced over your willingness to serve the Lord in such a sacrificial way."

There are a few coaching tips on using verbal confirmation to help your children keep on target:

1. Make verbal confirmation as soon as you can after the actual event.

2. Make the confirmation personal. Always use the child's name and make direct eye contact. Try to make physical contact: a hand on the shoulder or around the back.

3. Tell children how good you feel about what they did right and how it helps the family. Help them relate their behavior to the team.

4. Pause for a moment to let your comments sink in. This is a big payoff for the children. Let them *feel* the good feelings.

5. Always rave about the action, behavior, or character trait. Encourage them to repeat it.

6. Be specific. Don't be too general. By being specific, you build up tangible solid evidence that the child can file away for future self-confirmation. Specific details make good "heart-ware."

7. Avoid focusing on the "goodness" of the person. Children, like adults, are not always good, and they are very aware of it. If you keep telling them how good *they* are, it will confuse them, and you may lose a little credibility in their eyes. Keep giving positive confirmation for actions, thoughts, behavior patterns, and relationship skills. They will automatically make their own transfers to enhance their self-esteem.

This does not mean that you should withhold expressing love for them. Unlimited love should always be expressed even when they know they have done something wrong. When a child acts unlovable, that's the time he or she needs unconditional love the most. In fact, it's the whole point of unconditional love.

8. Try to weave your own opinions and feelings about the event. You are a "significant other," who acts as a testing ground on whom the child can experiment with behavior. If he or she discerns your pleasure and approval for an action, the child will assume that the action will also attract others.

9. Mealtime is excellent for verbal confirmation. I have made it a rule to give at least one verbal confirmation to everyone at the table at every meal. At our camp during mealtimes, I insisted that each counselor speak to each of his or her campers and give a positive stroke of some kind using the child's first name.

10. Be natural, authentic, and sincere. Think of something that you actually feel good about and use it. Don't be artificial. They can sense when you mean it. My children (my wife too) are particularly keen on spotting a genuine stroke versus one I am doing so I can check it off my "good shepherd list of things to do for the day."

11. Let the compliment stand alone. Beware of the "but" trap: the tendency to mix compliments and reprimands by saying, "Son, you did this well, but let me explain how it could have been better," or "but here's what you did wrong." Children will soon learn that your evaluations are like ice cream doused with Tabasco sauce.

12. Relate the compliment in terms that the child can understand.

Never underestimate the power of positive compliments. The Bible has much to say about this:

A soothing tongue is a tree of life, but perversion in it crushes the spirit (Prov. 15:4).

Pleasant words are a honeycomb, sweet to the soul and healing to the bones (Prov. 16:24).

Like apples of gold in settings of silver is a word spoken in right circumstances (Prov. 25:11).

Let no unwholesome word proceed from your mouth, but only such a word as is good for edification according to the need of the moment, that it may give grace to those who hear (Eph. 4:29).

SMOKESTACK FATHERHOOD

The *Queen Elizabeth* ocean liner, the great pearl of the Cunnard Lines, lay tired and aching in dry dock after years of grueling service in the Atlantic. They decided to give her a major face-lift and convert her into a floating hotel. As they hooked the cranes to the forward towering smokestack and began to lift it off, it shattered into dust. The engineers rushed to discover the problem and soon found that the smokestacks consisted of only thirty coats of paint. The three-quarter-inch steel plate had long since rusted out. Only the shell was left. The substance was missing; only the decoration survived.[6]

American fathers need more steel and less flaky paint. Fathers need more than a thin veneer of pretty fatherhood tricks to stand up against the modern threats to the family and the downward spiral of family trends.

When I open up and confess my weaknesses and sin to my children and ask for forgiveness for the mistakes I make with them, they don't think less of me. Their respect for me goes up. So does their trust. Transparency removes barriers and makes you less threatening. It opens the door to intimacy and trust, two essential ingredients for building a support base for children. For children to feel support, they have to trust you, and they can't trust you if you hide behind masks and play roles. A high-control father without transparency with his children will come across as a strict non-supportive parent, and we have seen the implications of this type of fathering.

Playing roles can cause children great difficulty and can lead to emotional illness. They see the real you with all your warts and the deception of your mask, and they receive a double message. This incongruence does great damage to children. They need a dad who is genuine: What you see is what you get. Be like Popeye: "I yam what I yam."

All children have a father-shaped hole in their hearts, which cannot be filled by a mask or an actor. Only Dad as he really is can quench a child's thirst for a drink of Dad. Your children need access to your heart, to your thoughts and emotions.

Silence is not golden—it is yellow. It is the college yell of selfishness. Dr. Ed Wheat has written, "Adultery has slain its thousands; silence, its ten thousands." Men, we need to take off our camouflage and let our families contend with the genuine article. A man's love for his family members and their love for him is only as genuine as his transparency. They can't love and trust whom they don't know, and without trust, discipline is a mockery. Unless you are transparent, they won't feel the support that makes discipline effective. Present your self, father, and let your family into your life.

DELICATE DELIBERATION

When Helen started the seventh grade, she began to show an interest in a tall handsome eighth-grade boy who had failed two years and had a reputation as a troublemaker. He paid a lot of special attention to Helen, and she became quite flattered. It didn't take long for one of Helen's teachers to call her in and advise her against associating with this boy and his friends.

A few days later, Helen approached me on the back porch of our country home and struck up a rambling, somewhat fragmented conversation. I soon realized that she had some serious things bothering her and tuned in to her alertly with all of my concentration. I let her play me out with her "testing" conversation, and I just listened quietly, asked questions, and let her know with my nonverbal communication that she had my utmost attention.

When I passed all of her little tests to see if I really cared and really wanted to listen, she told me the story about the boy and the teacher. "Daddy," she asked, "I wonder what you think about all of this?"

I kept calm and responded slowly. I carefully began asking her questions about her feelings and thoughts about boys in general and what she considered important qualities and traits in men. I then asked her, "Helen, how does this boy stack up against what you just told me your ideals are?"

As she answered that question, she talked at length. Then, after she had been led to make objective observations, she realized that she had been responding with her emotions and not her mind.

I asked her, "Helen, how can a boy so different from what you really want have such an appeal to you?" She struggled to find the answer. Suddenly, she saw it with great clarity. He trusted her as a woman and paid her close affectionate attention. This had been a new and very pleasurable experience for her, as well it should have been. The emotional electricity overwhelmed her good judgment, and she could not see the boy as he really was.

Helen quickly made up her mind to back away from this boy. She asked me how she could best go about it without hurting his feelings or making him mad. We talked quite a while and finally brought closure to the subject. That night at dinner, Helen seemed so cheerful and freed from the heavy pressure she had been under.

Here is a case study showing how a father can come to the aid of his daughter and gently counsel her with wisdom on how to deal with a serious issue. Helen had briefly lost sight of her target and could easily have veered off her flight path. I could have made the problem worse if I had stormed in with condemnation and ultimatums. I didn't lecture her or express disappointment. I didn't make her feel stupid or like a failure. I didn't let my fear and alarm show through.

I accepted her completely and simply asked questions that would gently lead her to "observe discretion" and let her articulate the answers — "her lips may reserve knowledge." I guided her, and she solved her own dilemma. I helped retarget her and at the same time, walked her through a thinking process that would help her retarget herself in the future.

E-TEAM HUDDLE GUIDE
CHAPTER SIX: DAD THE FAMILY SUSTAINER

E-TEAM REVIEW
10–15 minutes

Dad, the Family Shepherd

After coffee and fellowship, take 10–15 minutes to allow the men to tell about the results of last week's project. This is the accountability part. Be firm with each other and encourage everyone to complete the projects. If anyone encountered difficulty or had a family problem arise, pause to allow the E-Team to address the problem and pray.

E-TEAM DISCUSSION
50–60 minutes

This part allows you to discuss the key concepts in this chapter and relate them to your individual lives. Be sure to leave time to complete the Workout and Encouragement sections.

THE PRINCIPLES (Check the text for help.)
1. Discuss what it means to be an accountable father.
2. Define and describe the following four kinds of parents: Authoritative, Permissive, Neglectful, and Authoritarian. What are the two key elements that produce the best results in children?
3. Which coaching tip on confirmation meant the most to you and why?

THE IMPLICATIONS (Why are these ideas significant?)
4. Of the four types of parents described in the Support/Control Matrix, which one do you think is more prevalent in our society and what are the implications for our culture? What bearing will this have on your grandchildren?
5. Why is confirmation so important to a child? What is the difference between a child who has had adequate positive confirmation and one who has not?

THE APPLICATION (How do these ideas affect me?)
6. Locate your father in the Support/Control Matrix in Figure 25. How has his specific mix of support and control affected you today?

141

7. Locate yourself in the Support/Control Matrix in Figure 25. How is your specific mix affecting your children?

8. If your children were interviewed by a talk show host, how would they describe your style of confirmation?

E-TEAM WORKOUT
10–15 minutes

Allow each man to choose one of the project options (plays) to perform during the week. If so desired, design your own project. Note: It is essential that each man leave having made a definite commitment to a specific project.

1st PLAY:
Start a one-a-day program: Make a confirmation comment to each child each day.

2nd PLAY:
Make an appointment with your wife and teach her about the Support/Control Matrix. Ask her what kind of parents she had and how it has affected her. Ask her where she fits in the matrix.

E-TEAM ENCOURAGEMENT
5–10 minutes

Close the meeting in prayer for each other and your families. Include in your prayer a specific request for spiritual power to successfully complete your project.

BREAK THE HUDDLE, GO HOME AND RUN THE PLAY!

The Fatherhood Function:
To Tend

Chapter Seven
Dad the Family Motivator

TEACH		TRAIN		TRACK		TEND	
1	2	1	2	1	2	1	2

"Inability to be firm is the commonest problem of parents today. The basic trouble is the fault of the experts. It is a cruel deprivation that we professionals have imposed on mothers and fathers. . . . We didn't realize until it was too late how our know-it-all attitude was undermining the self-assurance of parents."
—Dr. Benjamin Spock[1]

POLE VAULTING IS THE PITS

Brandon entered the Arkansas high school decathlon at the end of his freshman year and placed somewhere around thirty-fifth out of eighty. Since the pageantry and challenge of the decathlon struck a fire in him, he set his goals to win it by his senior year. He labored with grim determination, and in his sophomore and junior years he moved up in the standings. Going into his senior year, he was selected by the papers as one of the top three favorites to win first place in this grueling two-day, ten-event iron man contest.

Unfortunately, Brandon underwent serious surgery a few months before track season. He had a 1/2-inch horizontal strip of bone cut out of both cheeks to correct a birth defect. He had his jaw wired shut for weeks and lost twenty pounds trying to eat through a straw. His strength and conditioning melted away. But he worked hard. Day after day he completed the track team workout and stayed late to perfect his decathlon events. After track season, under the broiling Arkansas sun, he toiled alone for his final decathlon.

The big weekend arrived. Brandon did well. After eight events, he and a couple of other athletes surged ahead of the pack. The suspense and pressure mounted. His most dreaded event, however, approached. Brandon stood at the start of a long asphalt runway and stared at his obstacle — a crossbar looming high above the pole vault pit. Traditionally his worst event, he always struggled to suspend his lanky 6'3", 200-pound frame at the top of the pole and thrust himself over the top.

He scratched on his first try. His steps were off, and he crashed through the pit with no lift at all. Only two attempts are allowed. The other men in his flight sailed over easily and increased the anxiety in Brandon. On his last try, he stood and stared at the crossbar, trying to picture his technique and success in an attempt to psyche himself up.

Four years of painful, sacrificial workouts flashed through his mind. It had come down to this one event and this one try. Another scratch and he would fall hopelessly back into the pack with no way to catch up, and with only one remaining event. He never wanted anything more in his life than to get over that crossbar.

Little did he know that in just a few minutes he would face a barrier in life far more formidable than that crossbar. It's one thing to get your body up off the ground and over a crossbar and another thing to get the pieces of your heart up off the ground and over the next step in life.

He started his run and picked up his stride halfway down the runway. He held his pole in a crossover grip. His face strained with effort. At the exact instant, he thrust the end of his pole into the slot at the front of the pit . . . and missed it! His pole tip skidded into the pit, and he flew through the air dangling from the pole out of control. He crashed into one of the standards at the side of the pit and rolled over a few times.

Sandy and I stood paralyzed, staring at his still form. He finally pushed himself up slowly with agony stitched on his face, not from the physical pain, but from the realization that he had scratched on the pole vault and netted zero points, which threw him out of contention. He would be lucky to place in the top fifteen now.

His eyes sought mine. When our gaze locked, he cried out, "Dad, I blew it! I lost! I failed!" He grabbed his head with both hands, reeled around, and bent over, sobbing. I dashed over to his side and gave him a big bear hug. We started walking away from the competition to the privacy of his track "camp" under the far bleachers. All he could do was keep mumbling about losing and blowing it. We found our mat and sat down. No words. Nothing could be said. Nothing to be done. Only pain to be endured.

PARENTHETICAL COACHING TIP

Never, never, never approach an athlete who has just been defeated and say any of the following:

1. "It's OK. It's just a game."
2. "It's OK. You did your best."
3. "It's OK. God is in control."

All the above may be true, but truth is not the answer to the agony of defeat. Time is. An athlete needs time. And understanding. It helps if you hurt too. Sports don't head the list in eternal values, but to a young athlete it's as big as life gets at his age. If you ever ask a defeated athlete the question, "What happened?" you should be forced to run 500 laps and do 1,000 push-ups. Just be there and care.

Figure 26

Obviously, Brandon had totally lost his "game face." He had come so far and done so well on an adrenaline high. This crushing defeat sucked all the competitiveness out of him. He simply wanted to withdraw. He had no fight left. He could not imagine running a mile, the last event.

After Sandy joined us, we just sat quietly together. Brandon was locked up in his own heart, where no one else could go. He drifted there all alone trying to stop the grief and come to terms with his pain. Gradually he recovered control. No way was he going to run a competitive mile. He kept saying, "Dad, it's no use. I can't win. I just don't want to run the mile. I lost. I'm finished. Let's go home."

Then, he lapsed into silence and kept glancing at me. "What do you think, Dad?"

"Well, Son, it's your choice. If you run it, it won't be to show a trophy. It will be to show your character. Here you are, after years of football and track, in your last high school athletic event. How do you want to go out? What do you want to remember? What do you want to show these coaches and decathletes? I feel like you do, and I understand. I wouldn't blame you if you scratched the mile. But, it's your choice."

About that time, Jim Brady, his track coach, came over and huddled up with Brandon for a few minutes. I saw Brandon slowly nod his head as Coach Brady told him that he still had a chance to place in the top ten if he ran a 4:53 mile. Then we left Brandon to let him sort out his heart.

A half hour later, I looked up and saw Brandon striding in the infield warming up for the mile. I went over and helped him stretch out. I walked with him to the starting line. He ran his mile. He showed his heart. He gutted it out and ran the fastest mile of his life. He placed 7th in the decathlon and has a trophy on the wall. But I have his gold medal for guts hanging in my heart.

After teaching, training, and tracking his children, a family shepherd must "tend" his children — to take whatever extra steps that are required to ensure success. This function of "tending your flock" is taken from Isaiah 40:11:

> Like a shepherd He will tend His flock, in His arm He will gather the lambs, and carry them in His bosom; He will gently lead the nursing ewes.

To tend means to retarget. It means to do whatever is required to ensure movement toward maximum success of those for whom you are responsible. A shepherd lovingly embraces his sheep and keeps them moving toward success. He broods over his flock and protects them from all outside dangers and from self-injury. He also makes sure they have food and water. He not only scrutinizes the sheep as they amble around his ankles, but his eye also scans the hills on the horizon, searching for the next feeding fields and fresh water. He pays any price to keep the sheep moving toward greener pastures.

A shepherd gathers his children, carries them, and leads them onward. Tending is doing whatever is required to shove your child over the top and on his way to excellence. It represents the last surge of effort required to put the polish on the child. You need to reach in and disrupt the problem that's nudging the child off course and make the necessary adjustments to realign the flight path toward the target. You need to tend your child.

Tending separates the dads from the duds. When a family shepherd finds his children veering off track, he must act. Even though it may not seem important or even if it causes a lot of disruption, you must act. You must make the necessary corrections to get them retargeted. Sometimes, it only takes a little nudge. Other times, it requires a big shove. Whatever, you must pay the price now to enjoy the benefits later.

> All discipline for the moment seems not to be joyful, but sorrowful; yet to those who have been trained by it, afterwards it yields the peaceful fruit of righteousness (Heb. 12:11).

This and the next chapter deal with the final step of equipping — to tend. This one presents coaching tips on how to motivate your children to do right. The next chapter deals with the techniques of discipline that correct your children when you catch them doing wrong.

First, let me make several important points about motivation:

1. Motivation boils down to self-motivation. Strictly speaking, you can't make anyone do anything; you can only create conditions for people and let them motivate themselves. Of course, putting an electric shock collar on a girl establishes a rather rigid condition that theoretically gives her a choice. If you hold a gun to a boy's left nostril, will he feel good about his freedom to choose? The coaching tips in this chapter represent some alternative forms of persuasion.

2. Motivation relates to tasks. It gives me a motive that compels me to action.

> Purpose calls.
> Vision inspires.
> Goals direct.
> Standards correct.
> Motivation activates.

3. Motivation must be personal. Children have many common needs that make it possible to employ the standard motivational techniques covered in this section. All children have unique needs that require specially tailored motivational techniques as described in

the next section. But, whether standard or special, all motivation should be directed to a single individual. You do not motivate groups. Motivation must be aimed at the individual. Treat each child as a special individual as you apply the principles of motivation and keep the developmental phases in mind.

CLARIFY NEEDS

To motivate your children, you need to make sure they have a crystal clear picture of their need. The sharper the definition of the need, the greater the motivation becomes.

As a quarterback, Brandon wanted to direct a potent offense and win football games. What he really wanted was to achieve the good feelings that come with victory, teamwork, recognition/attention, identity, and competence.

What I knew that he didn't know is that to gain the spoils of victory, you need to excel on each play. I knew I needed to motivate him to concentrate on maximum effort on each play. I also had more than football on my mind. To maximize his whole life, Brandon needed to learn the lessons of trying, of "putting out," of giving a task all you have.

All this requires an ability to persevere when things go wrong, or when you are exhausted (Fatigue makes cowards of us all—Lombardi), or when all hope seems gone. Brandon needed to learn to recover, and I had to make this need crystal clear to him so he would make himself learn it.

I worked backward from Brandon's overall life goals, distilling the principle to a simple lesson, to its smallest component. If you want to play a good game, each play needs to be played as good as you can. He clearly understood what I meant. He adopted my plan. He motivated himself to do whatever it took to maximize every play.

I capitalized on our common interest in football and used it to motivate Brandon to become a person who *tries* on all the little things. He learned to do each little part right in order to do a good overall job.

ALIGN REWARDS

To motivate your children, convince them that your map leads to their missing treasure. Lock on to what they already want and show them the connection between your plans and their desires.

I made it clear to Brandon that if he could learn the secret of recovery, he would have a better chance of getting the most yards out of each play. The greater the yardage, the better the chance for victory and its benefits.

Sometimes, you can provide immediate rewards that build great motivation to accomplish a task. If their rooms pass inspection, if they complete their homework, if they go through an afternoon without fussing, or if they do a special favor for another member of the family, give them recognition and praise. Many parents with younger children use charts with checks or gold stars.

FEED RESPONSIBILITY

To motivate your children, convince them you trust them with authority. Capitalize on their desire to develop independence and let them have all the rope they need to hang themselves. But if they start making a noose, take some away. How many times have you heard your child say, "Here Dad, let me do it"? Well, let him or her.

When Helen became interested in horses (at age three), I probably erred in allowing her too much authority over her involvement. On her first ride, I let go of her pony too quickly, and she flipped off backward. Through the years she has had a broken collarbone, a broken leg, and many other bruises and contusions.

But she always knew that her authority was real and not a sham. We let her stay right on the cutting edge of her ability to handle the responsibility. We used feeding and care of horses to train Helen on how to handle responsibility. She got up at 5:30 every morning to feed and saddle the horses for the campers. In the winter freezes, she carried hay bales out to the fields for the horses, who stood with their fannies facing north and the icicles hanging from their manes. She broke ice in the water holes. She shoveled sweet molasses feed and put out salt blocks. She searched the woods and swamps for lost horses. And we paid her $25 per month!

If I had wanted to teach Helen lessons on perseverance, do you think I could have ever forced her to take a job with that kind of responsibility and work? No way. So I found something that she already wanted responsibility for and kept feeding it to her.

ENSURE SUCCESS

To motivate your children, convince them that their goals are within reach. Help them establish realistic goals and ensure they have acquired the ability and resources.

Often, a child will be reluctant to tackle a task or pursue certain goals because of feelings of inadequacy or fear of failure. To disarm these hindrances, you need to make sure the task is doable and the child has the necessary skills and resources to bring to bear on the problem. Once a child understands how to do it and sees that he or she has the resources, the child can be much more motivated.

Failure can be extremely demotivating. It's your responsibility to do what you can to make sure that your children don't fail needlessly. Impossible goals and insufficient resources are silly reasons to fail.

> They say you can't do it,
> but sometimes it doesn't always work.
> — Casey Stengel

ALLOW FAILURE

To motivate your children, convince them that failure will not affect your love and acceptance for them. Rejection can devastate children and if you turn against them because of a failure, they read it as rejection. If your children perceive this as a pattern, they will not want to take initiative to do anything for fear of failure and the resulting pain of rejection.

In the case of Brandon's interception and loss, it was important to assure him that his mistake and loss were irrelevant to my love and acceptance for him. It's not enough to be silent after failure. If you go bananas with victory and remain silent after defeat, the child receives a loud message of rejection. You must be committed to strong overt expressions of love and acceptance after a failure.

This is not to say that failure should not hurt and not be costly. But failure carries its own painful consequences without you adding to them. Let failure and pain teach their own lessons. You must keep pursuing your child with aggressive love no matter what.

MATCH DISCIPLINE WITH MATURITY

To motivate your children, use discipline techniques that match their maturity level. Nothing demotivates more than disciplining a child with methods appropriate for someone much younger. Conversely, a young child can be overwhelmed if you use techniques designed for much older children.

In chapter 4, I presented a chart that explained the developmen-

THE CORRECTION TECHNIQUES
FOR EACH MATURITY GAUGE

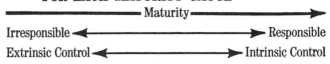

——————————— Maturity ———————————▶

Irresponsible ◀————————————▶ Responsible

Extrinsic Control ◀————————————▶ Intrinsic Control

CATEGORY	LEVEL I	LEVEL II	LEVEL III
MENTAL	Concrete Thinker	Logical Thinker	Conceptual Thinker
MORAL	Self-Focus Judgment	Others Focus Judgment	Principle Focus Judgment
BEHAVIOR	Control by Judgment	Control by Modification	Control by Perceptions
COOPERATION	Total Dependence	Careful Independence	Healthy Interdependence
DISCIPLINE TECHNIQUES	Pray Rewards Command Enforce	Pray Model Rules Power Lifts	Pray Dialogue Counsel Intervention

*COMMAND STYLE	Q1 Control Command	Q2 Convince Command	Q3 Consent Command	Q4 Concede Command

*(See Chapter 8 in *Dad, the Family Counselor*)

Figure 27

tal levels that a father can use to gauge the maturity of a child and thereby match the appropriate discipline measures. Here, in Figure 27, I show a portion of that chart with the correctional procedures that work best at each developmental level. The graphs show how the procedures are phased in and out thoughout the three levels.

Again, this chart shows general tendencies. It is not absolute and should not be followed rigidly. Your child exists as a unique designer child by the Lord and can't be crammed into a mold or chart. But this chart can help you keep from flying completely blind.

Another factor to consider here is that each child has different motivational preferences. Some techniques will not work on specific children at any level while some children require a standard power technique for all levels. It is absolutely essential that you know your child's temperament, motivational preferences, and developmental characteristics.

The chart does a good job of helping us see the need for flexible leadership and progressive discipline techniques. Notice how you start with basic control methods when the infant is in the instinctive Level I and continually progress through the range until the child reaches maturity and your role becomes that of a friend and consultant.

Be aware that things do not work as smoothly as the chart seems to suggest. Since there are spurts of growth followed by regression, the controls need to fluctuate accordingly. The basic rule here is to know your child and keep close track. Flexibility is the password.

MAKE IT FUN

The great value of sports and teamwork lies in their ability to simulate life and provide a great place to learn much of the "heartware" and "able-ware" of life, which is full of interceptions, fumbles, hard hits, losses, and penalties. Children learn a lot about teamwork, perseverance, and sacrifice. I used Brandon's games as practice sessions to teach him that "every play is a new game."

Since children love sports and games, why not take advantage of these activities and use them as training fields. Unfortunately, many fathers use sports to teach children the wrong lessons of life, like "You win or you die," "I love you if you win," and "Who cares if you win or lose as long as you look good?" Be sure to check your motives and the values you teach your children. You may have some blind spots.

On the other hand, take tedious chores and tasks and make games and sports out of them. Kids always prefer to play when they can, so why not make a game out of picking up their toys, cleaning their room, mowing the lawn, washing dishes, folding clothes, and doing the myriads of other projects around the house. One enterprising parent built a basketball hoop over the clothes hamper, and his small children loved shooting and dunking their dirty clothes into it.

DEMONSTRATE SUPPORT

Of course you support your children. You know that, but your children might not know it. I didn't realize my dad supported me until I was in my thirties simply because the things that he thought communicated support to me communicated something else. We didn't speak the same support language. Support must be demonstrated.

In *Dad the Family Coach,* I related the story about a special date I had with Helen when she reached puberty to make a point about family leadership. That incident also pointed out the need for close tracking. When Helen turned twelve, she started that difficult transition time for girls when their bodies start twisting and bulging, chemicals start secreting and flowing, and their interests turn from toys to boys. She bleated some warning signals that Sandy caught, and we decided it would be good for me to take Helen on a date. I took her out, and we had a fantastic date. She amazed me with her maturity and conversation level.

Our daughters crave our attention. They yearn for loving masculine attention from the dominate male figure in their lives. Our close association with them is absolutely essential for a healthy maturing process. We need to date and court our girls.

We need to condition them to the process of relating to a male who loves them and has their best interests at heart. They need to learn what it's like to go out with a man and enjoy a clean-loving relationship.

We had a small problem when Helen was twelve that could have led to something serious had I not squired Helen around Dallas on that unforgettable night. The problem here is that I was caught totally by surprise. I had no clue where she was or what she needed. Luckily, I have a wife who tracked our children and kept up with their development and needs.

GET REINFORCEMENTS

For many years, I taught that parents alone carried the responsibility of raising their children without any outside help. How foolish. The task is formidable. It takes all the help you can get. You need to network with your relatives, friends, youth director, and other children. Your family needs to weave its threads into the tapestry of the local Christian community. Ministry becomes a community affair, and the principles of "body life" impact your family and each member.

You need other parents. Helen will tell you that Mari Current and Sandy Perry significantly contributed to her life when she was younger. Then, in college at Fayetteville, the Jim Beckman family sort of adopted her. Brandon owes a lot to Mike Boschetti, a businessman in Little Rock. Mike met with Brandon and Isaac Jenkins for a 6:30 breakfast once a week for almost two years. Mike poured his life into those boys and taught them an incredible amount of biblical doctrine.

You need the college student ministries. I can't imagine a Christian attending college without getting involved with Campus Crusade for Christ, Inter-Varsity Christian Fellowship, Navigators, or other enthusiastic, well-grounded ministries. Sandy and I served on Campus Crusade for Christ staff for over twenty years and know from experience what it means to college students to have the support of a dynamic Christian student movement.

SEND YOUR KIDS TO CAMP

Without a doubt, Kings Arrow Ranch is the greatest help we ever had in raising Helen and Brandon. For ten weeks a summer for twenty summers, Helen and Brandon immersed themselves into a camp life brimming with some of the most outstanding college students in the nation. They attended every camp session until they were old enough to join the work crews. Then they worked their way up as counselors, program director, and finally Helen worked as girls' camp director.

Helen and Brandon rubbed shoulders with outstanding Christian students, who were incredible models. The college workers formed a ministry team to work with the campers. They discipled my kids throughout the whole year. They kept in touch. The great thing about camp is that you have young people just a little older than your children, whom your children can look up to. They live out the

Christian life in front of your kids and have fun. They reinforce with their lives at camp what you (parents—ugh!) have been trying to tell the critters.

TARGET EACH CHILD

Every child is a designer child and has his or her own individual, unique "bent," his or her needs and motivational preference. The above techniques generally work with all kids, but each child's individuality requires some special motivational techniques. Motivational techniques that work on one child may backfire on another. You can be trying your best to motivate your child while actually demotivating him or her.

Below are three motivational preferences and a description of the kind of person with whom they work best. These insights are from Pat McMillen, a visiting professor at Reformed Theological Seminary.

1. High-Achievement Person
   - Tends to spend time thinking of goals and how they can be attained;
   - Has an attraction for finding solutions to problems;
   - Enjoys taking calculated risks;
   - Seeks specific and concrete feedback on the quality of his or her work;
   - Eagerly accepts more responsibility and challenging tasks.
2. High-Affiliation Person
   - Tends to spend time thinking of warm, fulfilling relationships;
   - Promotes harmonious situations versus conflict within relationships;
   - Finds or desires satisfaction from being liked and accepted in the group;
   - Seeks situations that require working in cooperation with others;
   - Tends to make friends easily.
3. High-Influence Person
   - Tends to spend time thinking of how to influence others or how to control the means of influencing others;
   - Seeks positions of leadership in social or work groups;
   - Desires to give direction versus taking orders;
   - Tends to be verbally expressive and enjoys a good argument;

● Seeks high-status positions or positions requiring persuasive skills.

PREEMPT PROBLEMS

I've learned through the years that one of the best ways to motivate a family, a team, a board of directors, or a staff is to convince them that you know what you are doing, why you are doing it, and how it must be done. One of the things that bushwhacks morale quicker than anything is when a crisis or problem comes up and your followers find out you have no clue as to what to do. Then, when you make decisions under pressure, they are usually not as good as carefully prepared contingency plans. Your people soon lose confidence in you. So, do like Coach Tom Landry.

The legendary football coach of the Dallas Cowboys, Tom Landry, did not make decisions while pacing the sidelines. He treaded the turf watching the game. When a crisis demanded a response from him, he didn't decide—he remembered. He had already memorized computerized printouts of all tendencies, imagined everything that could possibly happen in the game, and had worked out a strategy for every contingency. When the unexpected happened, he simply called forth a decision he had already made in the calm of his office when he could afford the time to make careful, calculated decisions. Coach Landry primed himself for every game in this way.

A good father primes himself for child raising. The more decisions a father makes in a crisis and under pressure, the worse his record will be. A smart father thinks through as much as he can beforehand and establishes a plan. Then when he faces the opposition and things go wrong, he can bring forth his best possible solutions.

There are several major areas you should prepare for to be a good father: the cultural threats against your family and the volatile issues that tend to cause conflict.

Threats to the Family

Here is my list of major factors that presently contribute to the breakdown of the family. If you know about these things and keep them in mind as you lead your family, you can find ways to minimize their impact.

1. *Existentialism:* There has been an official break from traditional Christianity and an adoption of New Age existential mysticism.

2. *Statism:* There has been an erosion of the concept that government is an extension of family authority and an adoption of the idea that each citizen is an expendable/interchangeable ward of the state.

3. *Selfism:* There has been an embracing of the supremacy of the individual's needs over the welfare of the group to the point that we now live in a narcissistic culture.

4. *Androgynism:* There has been a drift toward androgynous gender roles that claim the sexes are identical rather than equal.

5. *Antigenerationalism:* The present generation represents the first generation to sever itself from genealogical lines by replacing parents with institutional groups and a commercial subculture. Childbearing has also been trivialized.

6. *Sentimentalism:* There has been a drift to replace a value system and family decision-making process that emphasizes pragmatic factors with a system that elevates subjective and emotional feelings as the prime consideration.

Causes of Conflict

What do parents and teenagers fight about the most? What can you anticipate and try to head off before things explode into a three-alarm fire? One study rated the adolescent responses to twenty issues that led to family disagreements and conflicts during the high school years. The results appear in Figure 28.

REMOVING A 275 LB. TACKLE

Perhaps the most discouraged I ever saw Brandon was when he walked on the football field at the University of Arkansas with dreams of becoming a great drop-back passer for the Razorbacks. Unfortunately, the Hogs ran the wishbone, which demands fleet-footed option quarterbacks, and they had signed five other great freshmen quarterbacks. It took about a week of two-a-days before Brandon called home to sadly inform us that he had been moved to offensive guard.

Offensive guard? Brandon, a 200-pound quarterback who had never blocked anyone in his life, now had to line up on every play and block down on a 250-pound nose tackle, or kick out on a 275-pound tackle, or pull and lead interference by running over a hostile 235-pound linebacker. How could I help my son?

Piece o' cake! Being a man of action, I dashed out a letter to Coach Ken Hatfield, athletic director Frank Broyles, and all the

CONFLICT ISSUES WITH TEENS[2]

Percentage of Male and Female Adolescents Rating Issues
as Leading to Family Conflict
Very Often While in High School

Issues	General Frequency	Males	Females
1. Going around with certain boys or girls	15.3	11.9	20.5
2. Boy-girl relations in general	8.2	3.4	15.4
3. Getting to use the car	13.3	16.9	7.7
4. Time spent watching TV	10.2	10.2	10.3
5. Eating dinner with the family	19.4	20.3	17.9
6. Being home enough	15.3	10.2	20.5
7. Responsibility at home	11.2	11.9	10.3
8. Money	7.4	3.4	13.5
9. Understanding each other	11.6	10.3	13.5
10. Disobedience	7.1	3.4	12.8
11. Quarreling and fighting	10.2	6.8	15.4
12. Ridicule of ideas	5.4	1.7	11.4
13. Arguing	15.8	12.1	21.6
14. Attitudes toward parents	7.1	3.4	12.8
15. Favoritism	5.3	.0	13.5
16. Rivalry between siblings	7.4	5.3	10.8
17. Schoolwork	7.4	5.3	10.8
18. Neglecting work	7.4	3.5	13.5
19. Religious or philosophical ideas	6.3	1.7	10.8
20. Church attendance	15.6	11.9	18.9

Figure 28

other coaches. I called the N.C.A.A. I held a meeting with the richest
men who donated funds for the athletic department. I published
letters in the newspaper. I, family shepherd extraordinaire, would
bring justice to my abused Heisman Trophy candidate. Up, up, and
away. I was rescue bound.

Well, not quite. I just listened to Brandon over the phone and
empathized with him. "Brandon, I know how you feel. I've played
the human dummy plenty of times in my career. I know you must
really be hurting." I continued to listen.

Of course I thought of little else for the next couple of days. I
prayed for Brandon constantly. We had both discerned it was God's

will for him to try out for Arkansas, and we both had confidence that he was where he was supposed to be. I didn't want to interfere with whatever process God had in store for Brandon. It was not appropriate for me to contact the coaches. Brandon and I both agreed that he faced a difficult situation that he would just have to work through. He knew he had to suck it up and go for it.

I decided to dictate my thoughts on a cassette tape and send them to him. I turned to the Bible to Acts 16, where it tells how the Holy Spirit led Paul to Asia and Philippi, where Paul lost his "position" as a speaker and was stripped and beaten, thrown into prison, and fastened into stocks. Paul could not have foreseen this turn of events. He had entered Philippi with optimism, thinking of success (Heisman Trophy?).

Paul, however, never gave up. In fact, he persevered with a good attitude even when the situation seemed pretty grim. Although he sat in jail filth with poor food and no sanitation, he started praying and praising God. Then God did a miracle. He sent an earthquake and opened the doors. As a result, Paul led the jailer to Christ.

I told Brandon how this passage applied to football at Arkansas. He had been led to Arkansas with optimistic hopes. Instead, his hopes were dashed. He lost his quarterback position, had been thrown into the guard position (prison and stocks), and received a daily beating with pads (rods). I told him that now he could prove his character to himself.

What would be his attitude during the hard times? Would he merely endure or would he persevere with class? Many of us have survived football. But could Brandon survive with a song on his lips and a hymn in his heart? Would Brandon get discouraged and become bitter and resentful?

Three weeks later, Brandon came home for the weekend, and we had a family meeting. I asked him what was the biggest lesson he had learned so far while at college. He responded with a smile and one word, "Humility." Everything had always come easy to Brandon. He had few failures. Now he had moved from hero in high school (started thirty-two games) to a human dummy in college.

He said that college football was the hardest thing he had ever encountered: not the physical part but the mental part—the humility and the pressure. He said he had wanted to quit many times but knew that God had some lessons for him to learn. He said the cassette tape I had sent him really helped him keep his perspective and keep going. He realized that if he didn't put out on every play that none of the other players would ever listen to him when he talked about Jesus Christ.

Brandon left home aimed at the target. He encountered some turbulence, and his feathers fluttered. After careful tracking, I tended to his heart to keep him going. I talked to him, listened to him, and shared some pertinent Scripture with him. Brandon heard and acted. He motivated himself, took off, and finished strong. He stuck it out for two years and gave it his best. He no longer plays for the Hogs, but he still wings his way toward the target of life.

E-TEAM HUDDLE GUIDE
CHAPTER SEVEN: DAD THE FAMILY MOTIVATOR

E-TEAM REVIEW
10–15 minutes

After coffee and fellowship, take 10–15 minutes to allow the men to tell about the results of last week's project. This is the accountability part. Be firm with each other and encourage everyone to complete the projects. If anyone encountered difficulty or had a family problem arise, pause to allow the E-Team to address the problem and pray.

E-TEAM DISCUSSION
50–60 minutes

This part allows you to discuss the key concepts in this chapter and relate them to your individual lives. Be sure to leave time to complete the Workout and Encouragement sections.

THE PRINCIPLES (Check the text for help.)
1. What are the best correctional techniques for children at Level I, Level II, and Level III?
2. What are the six major threats to the family?
3. What are the issues that most frequently lead to family conflicts with teenagers?

THE IMPLICATIONS (Why are these ideas significant?)
4. Why is it important to change correctional techniques as children move through different developmental levels? What happens to a child if you don't?
5. Many fathers find it difficult to know how to draw the line between being consistent/firm and being flexible. Many fathers want to know when to crack down and when to ease up. Discuss this problem using the principles in this chapter and examples from your family life.

THE APPLICATION (How do these ideas affect me?)
6. What motivational techniques did your dad use with you? Describe them, how you felt about them, and what results they had.

163

7. Consider the motivational techniques that you and your wife are presently using with your children. Evaluate them in terms of the principles in this chapter. Important: Do you and your wife have the same philosophy and use the same techniques, or do you disagree with each other and use different approaches with the children? Discuss the implications of this: How do the children perceive this and how does it affect them?

E-TEAM WORKOUT
10–15 minutes

Allow each man to choose one of the project options (plays) to perform during the week. If so desired, design your own project. Note: It is essential that each man leave having made a definite commitment to a specific project.

1st PLAY:
Make an appointment with each child and ask them to discuss the motivational techniques you are using with them. Ask for suggestions on how you can improve.

2nd PLAY:
Call a family meeting to establish a "conflict hit list"—a list of 5–10 things that cause the most conflicts in the family. Discuss the warning signals that lead to each of these conflicts and devise ways to preempt these problems before they get out of control. Preplan a solution for them.

3rd PLAY:
Make an appointment with your wife and evaluate your child motivational techniques. Define them, explain them, modify them, discard some, and add some. Continue until you come up with a system that you both agree on. Then commit to start using them and give each other permission to critique each other about them.

E-TEAM ENCOURAGEMENT
5–10 minutes

Close the meeting in prayer for each other and your families. Include in your prayer a specific request for spiritual power.

BREAK THE HUDDLE,
GO HOME AND RUN THE PLAY!

Chapter Eight
Dad the Family Restorer

TEACH		TRAIN		TRACK		TEND	
1	2	1	2	1	2	1	2

"Every child should have an occasional pat
on the back as long as it is low enough
and hard enough."
—*Bishop Fulton Sheen*[1]

GLASS IN THE GUTS

One fine crisp fall morning at Kings Arrow Ranch I was feeding the horses and making small improvements at the barn. Sandy interrupted my wrangler chores with shouts from the house. I darted out of the barn, charged around the lake to our home, and found Sandy outside holding eight-month-old Brandon in her arms. He had blood running out of his mouth.

"What happened?" I asked, as I grabbed and held him.

"He broke a glass," she said, "and before I found it, he had chewed and swallowed some of it."

I dashed into the house to the kitchen with him. I knew I had to make him throw up and discharge the glass. I sat him in his high chair and commenced to mix up a concoction made up of all the stuff in the refrigerator. I blended milk, orange juice, A-1 Sauce, soy sauce, a little mustard, and a raw egg for good measure.

Holding Brandon over the sink, I stuck the repugnant brew to his lips, pinched his button nose, and poured it down the hatch. He loved it. He cooed and gurgled. He wanted more. Failing in this fashion, I rushed into the bathroom with my baby boy, grabbed him by the ankles, turned him upside down over the commode, stuck my finger down his throat, and wiggled it to trigger his regurgitating mechanism.

I will always wonder what went through his brain at that moment. He sputtered, choked some, and, as if it suddenly dawned on him that he wasn't in the best of positions, he stared at me with two wide-open questioning, upside-down eyes. He probably thought, "Why am I hurting? The big guy has me. The big guy always means fun and excitement, not hurt. The big guy is hurting me! The big guy doesn't love me anymore. He has turned against me! What happened to my world?" And then, he panicked and started screaming and fighting back.

Watching him squirm above the commode in great pain, emotional anguish gashed my soul. Sorrow surged through me like a lightning bolt. This was my baby son. Bone of my bone and flesh of my flesh. He loved and trusted me so much. And I just knew he felt as if I had betrayed him and turned against him. I'm sure if he could have spoken, he would have said something like, "Now, Dad, I'm not sure this is the wisest way to handle this situation. I wonder if we could calm down and talk this thing over?"

I'm sure Brandon had serious questions about my love and support for him as he hung suspended above the commode. Actually, with him frantically trying to knock my hand away from his face and his jaws gumming my finger in a frenzy, I was in the midst of a significant demonstration of my love and concern for him.

I loved him far more than myself and would have gladly given my life to save his. I would certainly have risked his rejection of me in order to save his life. I knew he was hurting and unhappy, but I knew something else: It wasn't good for Brandon to crawl around with glass in his guts. I brushed aside all emotions in this crisis and did what was required for his best long-run interests.

Brandon had a problem that I needed to "tend" to. I went to a lot of unpleasant trouble to get Brandon to throw up. If he had been choking to death on food stuck in his throat, I would have taken a knife and opened up his throat. A family shepherd must do whatever is required to keep his children safe, secure, and progressing.

The same goes for misbehavior, which can be just as destructive to a child as physical harm. A child with dysfunctional behavior can be handicapped all throughout life. Just as Brandon had glass in his stomach that could slice him up on the inside, a child can get butchered because of problems in the heart that cause dysfunctional behavior.

This requires going the extra mile—to take the trouble to discipline your children. After you have loved, bonded, led, taught, trained, and tracked them, it comes down to putting the polish on. To finish out the child, you need to tend by nudging him or her on to obedience. Remember, the job description in the Bible for a child is to honor and obey parents while increasing in wisdom and stature and in favor with man and God.

There are many reasons for following through with firm discipline. Besides the fact that God commands you to do it, good discipline gives your child wisdom (Prov. 29:15), prevents the ruin of a child's life (19:18), prevents you from being shamed (29:15), and communicates love (Heb. 12:5-11).

This chapter treats the topic of serious discipline for children. How do you guide children to honor you by obedience? I look at it as using Teach, Train, and Track to aim and fire the child, while using Tend is to retarget the child if he or she steers off course. Tend is the correction function of child raising.

There are four levels of retargeting techniques that range from very mild to very severe. You don't want to sail in with a blistering spanking when the child is first inclined to do wrong. In order of severity they are:
1. Correction by command.
2. Correction by document.
3. Correction by consequences.
4. Correction by force.

Use command and document correction first. If that doesn't work, try consequential checks. Only as a last resort, use force. By force, I mean a spanking, which I call a power lift. A spanking is a power move that lifts them out of disobedience into harmony with right behavior!

COMMAND CORRECTIONS
This section will cover three kinds of verbal retargeting: Verbal commands, repetition, and wise counsel.

> And, fathers, do not provoke your children to anger; but bring them up in the discipline and instruction of the Lord (Eph. 6:4).

The Greek word translated as *instruction* here means to change behavior by the medium of communication. This retargeting technique doesn't depend on the authority of words alone; it implies the power of the nonverbal reinforcing the verbal to command a change in behavior. Studies show that the force of believability in spoken communication breaks down as follows:

1. Fifty-five percent of believability comes from the power of the nonverbal communication, such as body language, focused attention, and facial expression.
2. Thirty-eight percent of believability comes from the power of the tone of your voice.
3. Seven percent of believability comes from the words themselves.

You have probably heard the story of the boy who told his friend he had to go home after the thirteenth time his mother called for him to come home. When asked why now, on the thirteenth call, the boy responded, "Well, I can tell by the tone of her voice that she really means it now!" He had artfully trained his mother to call him thirteen times before he had to obey.

Command Voice

This takes me back to the "command voice" of Major Amos. Not one to risk a fate worse than death, I instantly plunged into my strict and rapid obedience mode when I heard the deep, rumbling bass-command voice summoning me to attention. God has given fathers a command voice endowed with father power. Use it.

It takes the same skill and effort to train a child to obey on the first command as it does on the thirteenth. It's funny how your child knew your command voice before you did. You have it, and you have already used it. Just be sure you train the child the proper response to it: Obey the first time.

A command is a command, not a suggestion. If it's a suggestion, say so. You certainly need a category of suggestions, nudges, hints, and encouragements. But you also need a genre known as "A Command That Must Be Obeyed and No Question About It." If it's a command, mean it and make sure it gets carried out.

Your command voice should be firm but not angry, harsh, threatening, punitive, or intimidating. You should speak with strong assurance and conviction fully expecting obedience. Don't let the child ever suspect any other option exists outside of quick compliance. Make your commands specific, clear, imperative sentences. Don't beat around the bush. Tell him plainly what you want. Describe carefully the behavior you intend him to stop or to do. Don't make him guess or leave room for him to wiggle out by claiming misunderstanding.

For nonverbal reinforcement, use clear eye contact, closeness to the child, and, if convenient, body contact like a friendly hand on the shoulder. It should be understood and acted on because of the foundation of love that you have already built. The child should learn to respond with respect because of your integrity, trustworthiness, and consistency, not out of fear or worry.

If the child does not respond to your command voice the first time, you need to employ the next level of retargeting techniques.

In addition to command voice, you have at your disposal other command features like:

Command gaze—that steady stare that bores into a child and sends clear but silent messages.

Command face—that look or expression on your face that sends warning signals to the child. (My wife has perfected "Command dimples"—when I'm in trouble she gets these two tight little dimples hovering around the corners of her mouth!)

COACHING TIPS ON
HOW TO USE COMMAND VOICE

1. Reprimand should occur immediately after the behavior if possible. The closer to it, the more it influences future behavior.
2. Remember the developmental ages and only reprimand when you know the child is capable of responding correctly.
3. Address only one issue at a time. A child cannot absorb the complete lesson if you dump more than one correction on him or her at a time.
4. Address the child in a normal conversational tone and not in anger. No matter how correct you are and how wrong the behavior is, the child will focus on the irrationality of your behavior instead of his or her violation if the child perceives strong anger. If you must, fall back, regroup, and approach the child later if possible.
5. Keep the child's identity and performance separate. Praise the child's personhood and critique the behavior. Don't label the child with bad behavior: "You are an 'F' student," "You are not an athlete," "You are a big baby."

6. Relate the reprimand to goals and success that interest the child. Avoid equating his or her performance with your prestige, reputation, or feelings. Don't say, "You know how this embarrasses your dad" or "What will our friends think?"

7. Phrase the reprimand in a way that helps the child gain insight into cause and effect. Guide them to the understanding that certain effects can be generated by specific behaviors. Leaving the child with insight and positive motivation for future behavior is much better than leaving the child in a cloud of guilt and gloom.

8. Phrase the reprimand in a way that instills in the child a desire to correct behavior because the behavior is wrong, not because he or she must perform for your love and approval. If your love is conditional, the child can develop into one of those miserable people who cannot handle mistakes or failure.

9. The more specific the reprimand, the more it develops intrinsic controls. The more general, the more the child learns extrinsic control and codependency.

Because specific comments direct the child to the behavior itself, he or she can adopt ownership of internal goals. Because general comments leave the child with ambiguous targets to internalize, he or she begins to look for vague feelings of approval that develop into outside dependency.

10. Beware of meaningless questions that lead the child to build a shame base and pain pool. The following questions are examples that build negative, defective self-esteem:

- "Why do you always. . . ?"
- "Why can't you ever. . . ?"
- "When will you grow up?"
- "How many times do you have to be told. . . ?"
- "What's wrong with you?"
- "Don't you know (understand, see). . . ?"

DOCUMENT CORRECTION

Kings Arrow Ranch, the camp Sandy and I founded and directed for twenty years, taught us incredible lessons about youth work and child rearing. I developed a slogan for one valuable lesson I learned while managing almost 100 college and high school students every summer: Write it down and throw it up. Write down every rule and procedure along with all consequences and corrections into a policy manual. Go over them with the students several times and ask them to agree with the rules and sign the document. Then, when anyone steps outside the "covenant of the document," you step up, put your arm lovingly around their shoulder, and throw up the document to them.

The document confronts them. The document condemns them. The document pronounces judgment on them. You are the friendly nurturing leader practicing management by document. You are a sympathetic nice guy, and the document takes the heat. If there is a problem, gather the witnesses, review the case, and throw up the document.

The document does not lie, play favorites, or take bribes. You are only showing them what they agreed would be just and honorable, and who would want to go against that?

CONSEQUENTIAL CORRECTION

Sometimes children need something greater than a verbal nudge. You may need to help them obey with physical assistance. One successful grandmother told me how she had to *help* her daughter put away her toys. She slipped her hands over the girl's hands like gloves, guided them to each toy, and helped her grasp it and carry it to the drawer. The girl resisted for a while, but, by golly, she did pick up her toys. She obeyed against her will. This method works great as long as you manifest greater strength!

Once as a six-year-old, I stole a thimble in Berlin, Germany. Mom had taken me with her on a trolley car ride all over Berlin on a shopping trip. The old city, still scarred and bombed out after World War II, fascinated me. Mom visited many tiny postwar shops, and in a quaint little one I found a small porcelain thimble and simply pocketed it.

Later at home, Mom spotted the hot goods and knew immediately that I had filched it. She hauled me right back across the city on the trolley and had me face the bespectacled old German clerk and confess my felony. It felt like the Nuremberg trials. I nearly died. But I never stole another thimble.

Better to use gentle, loving force and ensure obedience than allow children to grow up without any control at all. It's a lot better for all if you start your children off with power obedience rather than wait until they are seventeen and not have any options. They will be picking up far more significant and expensive things than toys if you don't help them master life at an early age.

According to what I have seen, those who plow iniquity and those who sow trouble harvest it (Job 4:8).

Do not be deceived, God is not mocked; for whatever a man sows, this he will also reap (Gal. 6:7).

Life carries its own disciplinary system called the law of consequences. Every action produces natural consequences. Each cause generates an effect. Many of these equations are so dependable that you can often induce desired effects by initiating the proper cause. When you have mastered these behaviors you are said to be wise. A wise father uses cause/effect principles to his own advantage.

The greatest source of dependable wise sayings can be found in the Bible, notably in the wisdom literature and especially in the Book of Proverbs. Many others can be learned by painful trial and error methods. Your job is to equip your children with a reservoir of this wisdom.

These cause/effect principles are your children's best teachers, and they are best learned when experienced. This makes them ideal for child raising.

Experience is an effective teacher. One of the most effective techniques of retargeting a child is simply to step out of the way and let nature run its course. This is what I call retargeting by consequential checks. You let the cause/effect principles of life check the child and make corrections. It takes the pressure off of you; you aren't the "bad guy." Also, cause/effect doesn't fudge or play favorites. If you stick your finger into the fire, you get burned, no matter how sincere or well meaning you are.

In child correction, a family shepherd can master two kinds of consequential checks:

1. Natural consequences — happen automatically.
2. Induced consequences — you cause to happen.

Natural Consequences

Helen drives somewhat in the way she keeps her room. She has a herky jerky style all her own. She never speeds. She just resents details — like watching the road. She reminds me of a pinball machine when she drives. She drove a twelve-year-old Datsun with bad paint, a horn that honked only when you turned the steering wheel sharply to the left, and a right back door that flew open on all left turns. Not her dream cool machine but good enough to serve as her bumper car.

I remember the first time I ever let her drive. We were in town, and I let her drive home. She drove sitting like a petrified mummy. When we arrived home, she got out complaining about how much driving irritated her eyes. Then she exclaimed that her eyes stung so much because she had not blinked for fifteen minutes.

One nice day she pulled up behind a giant purple Little Rock city garbage truck waiting at a stop sign. The traffic streamed by, and they waited. Finally the purple garbage truck decided to go for it. Helen likewise decided to bolt for it right behind the truck. Unfortunately, the truck driver proved to be a gutless wonder. Thoughtlessly he changed his mind and braked to a stop. The front of his truck slammed down on his front shocks, and his rear shot up conveniently for Helen to slip the Datsun's hood down underneath.

Helen sat stunned. She stared at the garbage in the back of the purple truck that pinned her car to the highway. Suddenly the purple truck darted across the road, made a left, and towed Helen's Datsun down the road. Helen kept jerking her steering wheel to the left to honk the horn, and the back door kept flapping open. All to no avail.

Helen had plenty of time to reflect on her driving habits as she rolled westward on Cantrell Road. Meanwhile, other drivers gazed quizzically at this strange spectacle. It looked as if the big purple garbage truck was having a little blue baby enroute. This was not Helen at her best.

Fortunately, the truck pulled to a stop to make a turn, and Helen's Datsun became disengaged. Helen pulled to the side of the road to watch the giant, wheeled grape sway on down the road— and to catch her breath. She took lots of deep breaths.

She didn't bother to tell us about this adventure until after she had totaled the little Datsun on the way to school one morning. She had tailgated a Jeep and rammed into it after it had stopped to make a left turn. A big Oldsmobile then plowed into the rear of her Datsun, and Brandon's breakfast flew all over him. Helen got out, called us, and refused to drive for almost a year.

Now, she has her own little car that honks without wrenching the steering wheel. She has improved 10,000 percent in her driving.

Natural consequences had taught her better than anything Sandy and I ever could have done.

Induced Consequences

Sometimes a misbehavior doesn't contain an automatic retargeting consequence. In that case, you must invent and induce a negative consequence that the child will logically connect with the problem. The child needs to realize that, when he or she commits a particular transgression, there will always be a price to pay. As the child learns to associate the negative consequence with the misbehavior, the child will mend his or her ways. Here are some examples of induced consequences:

● If your son marks on the TV screen with crayon, make him clean it off.

● If your daughter does not pick up her toys before going to bed, put them away for a couple of days.

● If your son watches too much TV and doesn't get his homework done, don't let him watch TV for a week.

● If your daughter doesn't get the dishes clean and puts them away still dirty, make her wash them again.

● If your son leaves your tools outside in the rain, don't let him use them for a while. (Brandon confuses tools with plants; he thinks tools need plenty of water and sunshine to stay healthy.)

● If your daughter gets up late and doesn't get ready for school on time, make her go to bed earlier for a couple of nights.

● If your daughter won't get ready on time (for a desired occasion), then cancel or postpone it or leave without her.

COACHING TIPS ON
HOW TO USE INDUCED CONSEQUENCES

1. It's OK to invent work projects for a consequence as long as the work relates directly to the problem and makes some kind of restoration. However, try to avoid using work projects as general punishment. For instance, if the child brings home a report card with low grades, don't induce a consequence of washing and waxing the car. The work clearly doesn't relate to the problem. The child can easily resent the work and build negative work attitudes.

2. Try to be consistent and predictable with induced consequences. After all, the purpose is to get the child to anticipate the price for

misbehaving ahead of time and thereby encourage positive behavior.

As with all rules, it would be best to write out as many of the policies and procedures as possible, including the induced consequences. This way, when you confront the child, you can hold up the objective, impersonal document and let it make the confrontation and specify the consequence. Your child will have difficulty transferring hostility and resentment to you if he or she is confronted by the document.

3. The induced consequences should be appropriate. They should be as serious as the misbehavior, but not extremely harsh or punitive. They should not be dangerous or in any way risk illness or injury.

4. Your attitude should be firm but sympathetic. You will probably lose points if they detect your glee or delight in their predicament.

FORCE CORRECTIONS — POWER LIFTS (SPANKINGS)

After you have exhausted every conceivable technique of retargeting, you may finally have to resort to serious correction by use of physical power to lift the child out of misdirection. I'm talking about spanking — power lifts.

The Power of Character

I call this form of retargeting a "power lift" instead of a spanking. I say "power" because the force of correction lies in the character of the parent and the seriousness of the misbehavior. It's not the spanking itself or the pain that should correct. It's the gravity of displeasing the integrity of the parent by moving outside the parent's limits of behavior. It's the injury to the wishes of the benevolent primary caregiver. A child should be grieved when bucking the power of authority of the parent. It's not the spanking — it's the power of personhood of the parent. It's who you are and what you stand for that counts.

This situation between a parent and a child coincides with what happens when a person sins against God. The power that corrects us should be the realization of how ludicrous our violation of the sovereign will of the Creator is, our holy, righteous, benevolent, eternal caregiving God. And how can we complain about the just punishments we incur for our infractions when compared to God's character?

I say "lift" because the purpose is to lift a child back up to the former high-flight path toward the target. Lift connotes the positive aspect. Your goal is not to beat the child down into submission but to lift the child up to eventual self-correcting control.

The Character of Power

To spank or not to spank—that is the question. The answer lies not in the spanking but in the character of the one who wields the power to spank. If the father operates within the chain of command from God to child with love and demonstrates godly character in his life, he or she has the authority to exercise power lifts. In other words, if a father has loved, bonded, lead, taught, trained, and tracked his child, he has got himself into position to spank the child as a last resort to keep the child on target.

Before you say, "Spanking is the refuge of the simpleminded," or "When the thinking gets tough, the tough start spanking," or some other comment that denigrates the concept of spanking, let me just say that I have heard and read it all before. I have studied both sides of this emotional issue quite well and come down on the side of spanking—but only under specifically defined conditions.

First of all, I vehemently reject any form of physical or sexual abuse, neglect, and/or cruelty. These subhuman practices have no place in the scope of child raising consideration. While we are at it, let's also condemn emotional, psychological, and mental cruelty. They can be just as damaging and life-ruining as physical damage. Emotional trauma can destroy the personhood of a child as much as physical harm.

I strongly eschew punitive physical, emotional, and mental methods of coercion, but I also scorn permissiveness and neglect. Simple neglect can injure children and cause them problems for a lifetime. *U.S. News and World Report* informs us of a national problem of spoiled children:

> Using the serious tone once reserved for childhood ailments such as diphtheria and measles, a recent article in a journal published by the American Academy of Pediatrics described a new illness sweeping the nation: The "spoiled-child syndrome." Children exhibiting symptoms of this disease are excessively "self-centered and immature," as a result of parental failure to enforce "consistent, age-appropriate limits." Often, the article goes on to suggest, spoiled children grow into spoiled adolescents and adults, never learning how to delay gratification or tolerate not getting their own way.[2]

The same article tells about the running debate over child-rearing philosophies and makes this interesting comment:

> Over the ages, child-rearing theories have changed as faddishly as fashions, reflecting a continual shift between viewing children as innocents who need little adult intervention and as inherently evil and in dire need of straightening out. Several recently completed scientific studies have provided the first objective test of which disciplinary styles work best, and all point in the same direction. Parents who are not harshly punitive, but who set firm boundaries and stick to them, are significantly more likely to produce children who are high achievers and who get along well with others.[3]

The wisdom of the world is relative, open to suspicion, and in constant flux. Take the world's most famous authority on children, Dr. Benjamin Spock. He taught many principles that contradicted the Bible. Almost two whole generations were raised by the gospel according to Spock. Now he says, "Inability to be firm is the commonest problem of parents today. . . . " We (secular psychiatrists and psychologists) didn't realize until it was too late how our know-it-all attitude was undermining the self-assurance of parents."[4]

With so much disagreement and vacillation among the experts and with child-rearing theories being invented and disproved as rapidly as computer software, no wonder a discussion on the topic can generate more radiation than illumination. One thing Americans do agree on is that, whatever we are doing, it's not good enough. A Louis Harris & Associates survey revealed that 64 percent of those surveyed believe parents just don't do a good job of disciplining their children.

Here's the big question: What theory are you willing to bet the lives of your children on? Are you going to rely on your own gut instinct? The methods your dad used? The latest *Psychology Today* pop theory? Think of what you are risking. As for me and my house, we will go with the ole reliable Bible. If I am willing to trust my eternal state of existence on the Scripture, I think I'll go along with it on spanking my children.

> He who spares his rod hates his son, but he who loves him disciplines him diligently (Prov. 13:24).

> Foolishness is bound up in the heart of a child; the rod of discipline will remove it far from him (Prov. 22:15).

The rod and reproof give wisdom, but a child who gets his own way brings shame to his mother (Prov. 29:15).

Spanking may run against popular notions of child-rearing, but let's face the gut issue square on: If worldly advice on child raising contradicts God's principles as outlined in Scripture, which way will you go? Remember, God's truths are absolute, trustworthy, and never change. What's more, they produce positive results.

How to Perform a Spanking

In her excellent book, *Discipline Them, Love Them,* Barbara Chase lists seven steps in the process of spanking:

1. Get alone with the child; do not publicly embarrass him.
2. Ask, "What is our rule?" You are making sure the child understood your instruction before you correct him.
3. Ask, "What did you do?" You are asking him to establish personal responsibility for his actions and confess.
4. Explain that you love him and equate love with correction.
5. Spank the child. Give him a few swift, but painful swats on the buttocks. The child's angry, mad cry should change to a softer, giving-in cry. You must learn to distinguish between sorrow crying and defiant crying.
6. Comfort the child immediately after spanking. Do not reject the child. Hold the child close and reassure him of your love. Only the parent who spanks is the one to do the comforting.
7. If necessary, have the child make restitution.[5]

COACHING TIPS ON
HOW TO SPANK A CHILD

1. Try to have all violations that earn a spanking written out beforehand so that you can refer to an objective document as your authority.
2. I tried never to discipline my children in public. I don't care how flagrant their violations, I tried to grin and bear it until I got them out of public. I think public humiliation and shame do far more damage than any transgression they commit or any gains instant discipline would provide. My grandfather beat my dad publicly, and I have been beaten in public. Believe me, you don't want to produce that kind of emotional trauma in your children. Public spanking is

damage enhancement, not damage control. Children should be controlled by your "command voice" or your "command stare."

3. Your attitude throughout the spanking should be one of serious firmness and sympathy for the child's transgression. Spank under control. Never spank in anger. If you are too angry, talk to the child and make a spanking appointment for later after you have cooled off. If you discipline in anger, the child leaves thinking how bad it is for you to be out of control rather than about his or her own transgression.

4. Spank for clear willful defiance, not for childish immaturity. For instance, if you leave your little son unattended while you are shopping and the toddler grabs an expensive display for balance, only to topple over with everything crashing down around him, that's your fault, not his. He only did the normal thing that all toddlers do. You should not put children in positions where they can easily fail and then spank them. If children don't know or couldn't help it, they don't fit into the retargeting category. They jump back into the teaching and training function.

5. Use spanking as a last resort and only for serious violations. (The more you use it, the less effective it becomes.) Make your shots count. I strongly discourage spanking after the child becomes eight or nine years old. Then they can began to control their behavior by perception, not modification. The child possesses the capacity to reason and negotiate by then, and the other methods should be effective enough. Never spank an infant younger than eighteen months old. A light tapping on the back of the hand mixed with your "command voice" should be adequate.

6. Spanking should be a management retargeting exercise and kept out of the arena of anger, temper flares, excessive punishment, and child abuse. You should never lose control and lash out with a slap or punch. It should be associated with love throughout the whole spanking process.

7. Spank with an inanimate object that will not cause any harm. Do not use your hand or any of your personal belongings like your belt. Use a designated spanking paddle. Never use your foot or shoe. You don't want the child to associate you or any of your personal effects with the pain.

8. Spanking should be done as soon after the violation as possible. If you wait longer than a few minutes with a young child, they may not make the association. But remember, don't spank in public or in

anger. Get alone and calm down before you spank.

9. Don't overcorrect. Too many spankings can be a warning signal that something is wrong with your overall child-rearing methodology. Backtrack and ask, "Is there something we are doing that is causing a high violation count?" Go back through the Four Fatherhood Functions and see if you are leaving out any ingredients.

WHAT CHILDREN CAN OVERCOME

As this book draws to a close, let me encourage you with this: Children can overcome almost any mistake in corrective technique as long as they know your heart is right. If you are in a chain of command, demonstrate love to them, cultivate transparency with them, have realistic expectations for them, and are consistent with them, you have already won the battle of discipline and correction. Conversely, your methodology can be immaculate, but if your heart is cold, selfish, masked, demanding, and inconsistent, you will most likely provoke your child to anger.

Child raising is heart management. If you get your heart right, your children will turn out all right.

E-TEAM HUDDLE GUIDE
CHAPTER EIGHT:
DAD THE FAMILY RESTORER

Dad, the Family Shepherd

E-TEAM REVIEW
10–15 minutes

> After coffee and fellowship, take 10–15 minutes to allow the men to tell about the results of last week's project. This is the accountability part. Be firm with each other and encourage everyone to complete the projects. If anyone encountered difficulty or had a family problem arise, pause to allow the E-Team to address the problem and pray.

E-TEAM DISCUSSION
50–60 minutes

> This part allows you to discuss the key concepts in this chapter and relate them to your individual lives. Be sure to leave time to complete the Workout and Encouragement sections.

THE PRINCIPLES (Check the text for help.)
1. Discuss the coaching tips on Command Correction.
2. Describe the two kinds of Consequence Correction.
3. Discuss the coaching tips on spanking.

THE IMPLICATIONS (Why are these ideas significant?)
4. What common problems can be solved by the use of correction documents?
5. What is the major difference in the correction philosophy of the last generation and the one of your generation? What is the difference in their correction techniques? What is the difference in their results?
6. What are all the dangers connected with spanking? What are the dangers of not spanking? In the debate over spanking, what is the one overwhelming reason in support of spanking?

THE APPLICATION (How do these ideas affect me?)
7. What major correction techniques have you been using with your children? What new ones do you need to incorporate and/or which ones do you need to improve on?

181

8. Do you and your wife agree on correction policy? Discuss this.
9. Discuss the reasons why your E-Team should continue to meet. Establish a plan for a break and a new course.

E-TEAM WORKOUT
10–15 minutes

Allow each man to choose one of the project options (plays) to perform during the week. If so desired, design your own project. Note: It is essential that each man leave having made a definite commitment to a specific project.

1st PLAY:
Pray about your E-Team. Should you stay together and take another course, or should you each become an E-Team Captain, start your own E-Team, and take them through the Dad the Family Shepherd Series? What are the advantages of staying together and how can you help fulfill Malachi 4:5-6 in America by starting your own E-Team?

2nd PLAY:
Make an appointment with your wife and evaluate your child discipline philosophy and strategy (you have one whether you have talked about it or not). Decide on three practical ways that you can improve it. Establish a monitoring system that will allow you and your wife to continue upgrading your discipline methodology.

E-TEAM ENCOURAGEMENT
5–10 minutes

Close the meeting in prayer for each other and your families. Include in your prayer a specific request for spiritual power to successfully complete your project. Also, pray about whether you should continue this E-Team and start another course or whether you should recruit your own E-Team and take your men through the Dad the Family Shepherd Series.

BREAK THE HUDDLE, GO HOME AND RUN THE PLAY!

The Extra Point

Dear Father,

Congratulations! You have just finished the Dad the Family Shepherd Series on fatherhood and therefore deserve recognition for your demonstration of commitment to your family. I think you ought to let your wife take you out to a special dinner to celebrate your achievement. Go for it!

As we close out the last of twenty-four E-Team lessons, I want you to consider this: your children can be best helped when you go far beyond book study and attach yourself to a long-range E-Team. Belonging to an E-Team gives you access to a committed family problem-solving team that can help you make the best decisions and do the right thing by your family for years to come.

An E-Team helps you keep your focus on your family and provides you with the encouragement and accountability which we all need occasionally. It keeps you on the cutting edge with the changing needs of your children.

Now that you have reached this milestone in your fatherhood enhancement process, I challenge you to ratchet up your involvement with Malachi 4:5-6 — to restore the hearts of the fathers in the nation to their children. You can make a dramatic impact in the lives of other men in your circle of influence if you help them with fatherhood.

Here are several suggestions that will help you with your own fatherhood and be a great asset to other men also:

1. Start your own E-Team and take your men through the Dad the Family Shepherd Series.
2. Schedule the Dad the Family Shepherd Video Conference in your church.
3. Help your church start an ongoing fatherhood training process like the Fatherhood Institute.

If enough men like you take Malachi 4:5-6 seriously, we will see a reversal of the trend of fatherhood deterioration in our nation. If we each do what we can, we can do what it takes to raise the profession of fatherhood to the lofty status God intends for it.

Thanks for your commitment and your achievement to date. Don't stop. Keep fighting for fatherhood.

Sincerely,

Dave Simmons

Endnotes

Scouting Report

1. Daniel Webster, *A Generation at Risk* (Chicago: Moody Press, 1990), 120.
2. David Blankenhorn, "Male Flight," *Minneapolis Star Tribune,* 7 November 1990.
3. Bill Parkinson, "Staubach and Namath," Church Sermon, First Baptist Church, Little Rock, Ark., Dec. 15, 1991.
4. Ken Canfield, "Trends of Bad News," National Center for Fathering.
5. "One Day in the Life of America's Children," Children's Defense Fund, 1990.
6. H. Stephen Glenn and Jane Nelsen, "Major Transitions in Lifestyle," *Raising Self-Reliant Children in a Self-Indulgent World* (Rocklin, Calif.: Prima Publishing and Communications, 1989), 30–31.
7. Ibid., 18–19.
8. Ted W. Engstrom, *The Fine Art of Mentoring* (Brentwood, Tenn.: Wolgemuth and Hyatt Publishers, Inc.), 4.

Chapter One

1. Rudolph Dreikurs, *Social Equality: The Challenge of Today* (Chicago: Contemporary Books, 1971).
2. Robert Lewis, "Magic, Get Real," Excel Newsletter, Dec. 9, 1991.
3. Glenn and Nelsen, 15.
4. Eric Hoffer, Ibid., 13.
5. Stephen R. Covey, *The 7 Habits of Highly Effective People* (New York: Simon and Schuster, Inc., 1990), 23–24.
6. Glenn and Nelsen, 52.
7. Frank Koch, *Proceedings — United States Naval Institute,* cited by Stephen R. Covey, 33.

Chapter Two

1. Oliver Wendell Holmes.
2. Jim Burton, *Baptist Men* (Newsletter), Jan. 22, 1990.
3. Howard G. Hendricks, Class notes, Dallas Theological Seminary, 1974.
4. Glenn and Nelsen, 53.
5. "How to Raise a Perfect Kid," *Esquire,* Nov. 1989, 122.

Chapter Three

1. Covey, 71.
2. Ibid.
3. Dr. Howard G. Hendricks, Class notes, Dallas Theological Seminary, 1975.

Chapter Four

1. Sandy Simmons, my wife.
2. Louise Bates Ames, Cofounder, Gesell Institute of Human Development, *USNWR*, 1984, 49.
3. Dr. Sid Crosby, Unpublished notes, 1991.
4. Josh McDowell and Norm Wakefield, *The Dad Difference* (San Bernardino, Calif.: Here's Life Publishers, 1989).

Chapter Five

1. Howard Hendricks, from the Foreword to *Dad the Family Mentor.*
2. Blanchard and Johnson, 79.
3. Carlson Learning Company, 1991.
4. Donald Helms and Jeffrey Turner, *Exploring Child Behavior* (New York: Holt, Rinehart, Winston, 1981), 394.

Chapter Six

1. The Institute of Human Development at the University of California at Berkeley, cited by *U.S. News and World Report,* Aug. 7, 1989, 50.
2. Jeannie Williams, "Michael Jackson," *USA Today,* Oct. 13, 1991.
3. Nancy DeMoss, *Spirit of Revival,* June 1988, 14.
4. Dennis Guernsey, *Family Life Today,* Jan. 1975, 7.
5. *U.S. News and World Report,* Aug. 7, 1989, 50.
6. *Leadership Journal,* Fall 1983, 87.

Chapter Seven

1. Dr. Benjamin Spock, *Family Concern,* Jan. 1981.
2. Helms and Turner, 389.

Chapter Eight

1. Bishop Fulton Sheen.
2. *U.S. News and World Report,* August 7, 1989, 49.
3. Ibid.
4. Dr. Benjamin Spock, "Spanking," *Family Concern,* Jan. 1981, 132.
5. Barbara Chase, *Discipline Them, Love Them.*

Appendix A

Dad, the Family Shepherd

E-TEAM

Review of Volume One and Overview of Volume Three

This book, *Dad the Family Mentor*, is the third of three volumes in the Dad the Family Shepherd series and should be read only after first reading Volumes 1 and 2, *Dad the Family Coach* and *Dad the Family Counselor*. Much of the meaning, even the selection of topics, of this volume will make sense only after reading the first volume.

To help put this volume in context, I have included this short review of the main ideas in Volume 1, *Dad the Family Coach*.

SERIOUS FATHERHOOD
(Volume One—Chapter 1)

Fatherhood has awesome significance outside our own personal experience and interests. Fatherhood is a central theme of the Bible. God tells us that the performance of fatherhood plays a major role in His plan for the ages and for the health and safety of individual nations.

Fatherhood is the means by which God intends the truth about Himself to be passed down through the generations. He has given fathers the assignment and the unique, mysterious ability (Father Power) to carry out this plan. God gave men Father Power in order to transfer the Gospel down through at least four generations of their descendants.

The Fourth Generation Rule does not distinguish between good and evil. The energy of Father Power picks up the heart of a man, good or evil, and hurtles it down through his seed. Father Power, therefore, can act as a negative force or a positive force. A father can send the light of God down through the next four generations, or he can send the darkness of sin down through the next four generations.

As Dad the Family Counselor, you must understand Father Power, the Fourth Generation Rule, and the dynamics of how your fathering style stimulates children the way it does, and use it to advantage with your family.

COORDINATED FATHERHOOD
(Volume One—Chapter 2)

Each family is a living organism, a unique entity, a personal life-form with a distinct personality and character derived from its two major components—the roles (the people) and the rules (the systems). Each family exists as a unique entity with its own identity, character, social system, structure, secrets, rules, ethics, and habits. Each one has its own way of facing adversity, coping with stress, resolving conflict, solving problems, and defending itself. Each one has its own habits of hygiene, recreation, and revitalization. They all age and die in their own way. Together, these elements give the family its own peculiar personality.

The family gets its personality from the members and the members get their personality from the family. The family is both cause and causal: the members contribute to the formation of the whole and the whole clearly marks the individual. Yet each individual is unique and self-contained with personal identity and boundaries.

Any force that touches one part causes an energy transfer to all other parts and change results throughout the whole structure. There is no independent action and no isolated unaffected parts. The whole works its will on each part and each part determines the whole.

Healthy families allow each person to develop uniquely and reach full interdependent maturity. Dysfunctional families blur the distinction between members and clump together in unhealthy codependency. They all stay caught up in each other's dysfunctions.

SPIRITUAL FATHERHOOD
(Volume One—Chapter 3)

There are two sides to fatherhood: Who you *are* and what you *do*. Your character and personhood matters more than your fathercraft and daddy techniques. A family shepherd is careful to *BE* the right man as well as *DO* the right things.

The Bible points out this double responsibility clearly in Psalm 78:72—"So he shepherded them according to the integrity of his heart, and guided them with his skillful hands."

Competent shepherding entails two essential aspects: your heart and your skills. You must have a heart of integrity, that is, you must BE a certain kind of man. You must DO specific activities that require a skillful hand.

It's not enough to just tackle the skills and techniques and bypass the development of your character. A man can be dysfunctional and master the Four Fatherhood Functions, then wonder why his family comes crashing down around him.

I give you now a major point of my concept of fatherhood: Children do what you are, not what you say. Who you are, the kind of man you are, is more important than all of your tasks, techniques, and talks. Children play with your words but work off your heart. Out of your heart come the issues of life and that's the true source of wisdom to a child.

You need to make sure your heart is right with God. You must know God personally through Jesus Christ and allow His Spirit, the Holy Spirit, to change your heart and empower you to reach your full potential for fatherhood. The best father you can be is the best son you can be. You must be a son of God to be the best father for your child.

RESPONSIBLE FATHERHOOD
(Volume One—Chapters 5-8)

Many fathers are demoralized because they can't get a grip on the overall scope of fatherhood and what their responsibilities are. No father can feel secure unless he knows exactly what he is supposed to do, how to do it, and how well it must be done. Therefore, I have gleaned from the Scriptures, condensed all the tasks of fatherhood into four major groups, and formatted them into a Fatherhood Job Description that has two major components—fatherhood style and fatherhood functions.

The Fatherhood Style
The Bible predicts that certain styles of fatherhood automatically produce confusion and rebellion. This passage explains what happened between Dad and me. "And, fathers, do not provoke your children to anger; but bring them up in the discipline and instruction of the Lord" (Eph. 6:1-4).

I have paraphrased this passage to read like this:

Fathers, don't use a command style that frustrates your children and incites them to automatically rebel against you and your value system and spin out of control. Instead, use God's wisdom, be personally involved, and use proper command style to nourish them up with biblical principles of discipline and motivation.

The Fatherhood Functions
The Dad the Family Shepherd job description presents the Four Fatherhood Functions. These functions and the roles are listed below.

Chapter	Function	Role
Five	To Love	Dad the Family Priest
Six	To Bond	Dad the Family Coach
Seven	To Lead	Dad the Family Man
Eight	To Equip	Dad the Family Mentor

Volume 1, *Dad the Family Coach* gives introductory material on each of these functions. Volume 2, *Dad the Family Counselor* expands the first three and gives detailed coaching tips and techniques, while this book, Volume 3, *Dad the Family Mentor* does the same for the fourth function—To Equip.

A BRIEF SYNOPSIS OF THE FATHERHOOD FUNCTION: TO EQUIP

SYNOPSIS OF "TO EQUIP"	
Function	To Equip
Role	Dad, the Family MENTOR
Benefit	COMPETENCE
Penalty	DEPENDENCE
"To Equip" answers the child's question: "Can I do it?"	

Equipping is the diligent labor that provides children with the right environment and enlightenment required to cope successfully with life. The father has the primary responsibility to provide everything a child needs to reach maturity in a healthy productive way. He must provide the right environment that allows maximum growth, and he must provide the right enlightenment to help the child learn to cope. He does not have to do everything himself: He can delegate, but he must assume the responsibility that it will be done.

THE ROLE: DAD THE FAMILY MENTOR
As Dad the Family Mentor, you transfer the skills of competence to them. You help them master the trait of being effective (doing the right things) and efficient (doing

things right). Your charges emerge from your attention able to cope with life successfully. They become achievers.

THE BENEFIT: COMPETENCE

Research shows a powerful relationship between the involvement of the father and the competence level of the child. Task-oriented fathers push children (boys and girls) to expand boundaries, experiment, take risks, and overcome obstacles to be successful. Relationship-oriented mothers emphasize rapport and sensitivity with people. A strong dad, to a child, is the agent of instrumentality. Involved dads inspire children to effectiveness and efficiency. Children learn to cope with life much better with an involved child-friendly father.

THE PENALTY: DEPENDENCE

Almost all research shows that paternally deprived children do not compare favorably in any positive area to children with strong fathers. The one word that best characterizes fatherless children is dependence. They do not cope with life well and depend on others to meet their physical, emotional, and psychological needs. They invariably form discordant relationships and dysfunctional families.

Appendix B

Dad the Family Shepherd Conference

The Dad the Family Shepherd Conference is an 8-hour presentation of a systematic theology of Christian fathering. This conference has been presented to tens of thousands of men since 1984, both in live and video format.

The live conference requires a minimum attendance of 300 men. The host church or group must organize and promote city-wide and involve a number of churches in the process. There is a limit of 18 live conferences per year. The video conference has no minimum number of men and is available to schedule any weekend.

The conference, entitled *Build Your House on the Rock*, covers not only fatherhood, but other critical issues men must face. It contains these messages:

FATHER POWER:	How to build a Christian dynasty
LOVE UNCHAINED:	How to make love realistic
THE MASTER PLAN:	How to build family teamwork
HONOR THY WIFE:	How to please your wife
3-D SEX	How to enhance your wife's sex life
MISSION CONTROL:	How to balance your priorities
CHILD SECURITY:	How to build child security
CHILD MANAGEMENT:	How to increase child confidence

HOW TO SCHEDULE A CONFERENCE

1. Evaluate the state of fatherhood in your community and pray about getting involved in promoting Christian fatherhood.
2. Contact the Dad, the Family Shepherd office for more information and ask for the 14-minute promo video that highlights the conference. Contact:

Dad, the Family Shepherd
P.O. Box 21445
Little Rock, AR 72221
(501) 221-1102

3. Take the material to your pastor and start the process.
4. Call the DFS office with your date.
5. Dad, the Family Shepherd then provides comprehensive training material to organize your men to host a conference.

Appendix C

Mission Statement
for a Father

A fatherhood mission statement (FMS) gives you a precise statement of what you want your fatherhood practice to accomplish and sets forth an unchanging standard, or constitution, that will best ensure the achievement of your mission. It will function as a document that keeps you on track by providing objective criteria for making judgments and decisions. It is your fatherhood North Star.

There is no universal FMS because such a statement should flow out of the individual father's heart. Each father should craft his own. Then, recraft it through the years because it should be somewhat flexible, not chiseled in concrete. As you mature and gain more wisdom, it will reflect in your FMS.

Even though each FMS will be unique, there are some standard elements which should be included:

1. A statement of your core identity.
2. A statement of fatherhood purpose.
3. A statement of fatherhood character.
4. A statement of fathering principles.

My suggestion is to designate a morning alone to work out a rough draft of a FMS. Put it aside for a few weeks and work on it again. Then, run it by your E-Team or a few of your best friends and get their input on it. Finally, polish it up, get it typed, and post it in a place where it will serve as a constant reminder.

Here is an example of a fatherhood mission statement that you can use to help you get started on your own.

MY FATHERHOOD MISSION STATEMENT

My Identity
Because of Christ's redemption, I am a new creation, a child of light and of infinite worth, and, as a son of God, I am deeply loved, completely forgiven, fully pleasing, totally accepted, and absolutely complete in Christ. I am a man with Christ in the center of my heart, and all of life's issues flow out of and revolve around this fact.

My Fatherhood Purpose
My role as a Christian father is to help fulfill the Great Commission (Matt. 28:18-20) by:

1. Functioning as the head of my family.
2. Creating an environment where my children can become capable productive citizens and realize their full potential for God.
3. Transfering the truth about God down through the next four generations of my descendants.

My Fatherhood Character
My desire is to become a man with the following traits:
1. A man secure in my identity in Christ with my heart yielded to Him.
2. A man dedicated to demonstrating the fruit of the Holy Spirit in my life (Gal. 5).
3. A man with a shepherd's heart for my family who seeks to be an example and not lord it over others.
4. A man responsible for my own life and able to subordinate my behavior to timeless values and principles rather than being controlled by external people, events, or situations.

My Fathering Principles
I am committed to abiding by the following principles:
1. To live under authority and function in an accountability system which includes God, the Bible, the leaders in my church, my board of directors, and my E-Team.
2. To pursue my lifetime purpose of serving God by subordinating the issues of my life to that purpose and keeping my twelve major priorities balanced with special emphasis on the relationships with my family members.
3. To seek consistent spiritual input from the Scriptures and other godly friends and teachers.
4. To love, bond, lead, and equip my family to the best of my ability.
5. To balance tasks with relationships and abide by the Protestant work ethic of seeking to be effective and efficient in all areas of my life.
6. To consistently seek outside, objective, competent input on the issues and problems in my family so I can arrive at the best possible decisions, solutions, and resolutions.
7. To make each child a field of lifetime research and study in order that I might serve him or her with excellence.
8. To make fatherhood a field of lifetime research and study in order to stay on the cutting edge with my role and performance as a father.

Appendix D

Family Profile Instruments

Both of these instruments may be ordered from Dad the Family Shepherd.

THE PERSONAL FATHERING PROFILE

The Personal Fathering Profile (from the National Center for Fathering) represents a major breakthrough in the field of fatherhood enhancement. This psychometric instrument provides you with a comprehensive fourteen-page computerized report on your personal unique fathering style as it pertains to the four fathering dimensions, the twelve strong father factors, and the four personal fathering satisfactions.

The PFP gives you feedback on where you are on a continuum on each of the four fathering dimensions:

> Your Fathering Awareness
> Your Fathering Involvement
> Your Fathering Consistency
> Your Fathering Nurturance

It also lets you find out how you are doing in each of the Twelve Strong Father Factors—characteristics which all strong fathers share in common.

The PFP comes with a seven-week E-Team course so you and your friends can take the PFP, get it interpreted, and spend seven weeks discussing how to enhance your fathering style by using this scientific fathering tool.

THE CHILD DISCOVERY PROFILE

The Child Discovery Profile (from the Family Discovery Network) will allow you to analyze the temperament of each of your unique children from four years old and up, and provide an exhaustive explanation on how they relate to other family members and respond to parents. It is a self administering, self-scoring, and self-interpreting instrument based on the concept of four personality types and will reveal the following on each child:

1. Degree of people/task orientation
2. Degree of active/passive orientation
3. Greatest strengths
4. Natural limitations that need correction
5. Communication style
6. Social and personal fears and apprehensions
7. How behavior changes under pressure
8. Philosophy of money
9. Decision-making style
10. Greatest needs
11. Recovery preferences

Appendix E

Teaching with
Word Pictures

Word pictures enhance learning by making principles precise, poignant, and applicable. They also communicate on an emotional level which drives truth deeper into the mind. For example, which do you think would best motivate a child to work steadily, a or b?

    a. One should take care not to procrastinate when pursuing a goal. Steady consistent progress offers better assurance that one will accomplish one's goals with efficiency and effectiveness.
    b. The story of the Tortoise and the Hare.

Here are some other examples of principles with word pictures to help drive them home:
    1. Once you say something, you can never take it back. It's like squeezing toothpaste out of the tube.
    2. For a family to be strong, all members must hold on to each other. A chain is only as strong as its weakest link.
    3. Love is sacrificial action. Sandy gave Dave the best steak dinner. Helen gave Brandon her quarter to go to the petting zoo. (See chapter 5 in *Dad the Family Coach*).
    4. Women are more holistic and have a broader range of communication than men. Women speak in spider webs and men speak like knotted ropes.
    5. Fathers are supposed to pass the Gospel down through their descendants. The truth of God is an arrow shot from the bow of the prophet that hurtles down through the corridors of time. It is a river that cascades down through the generations and splashes around the world.
    6. Quality time with kids demands a quantity of time. Kids are like little birds in a nest: you need to be standing there with a worm for those special times when they open their mouths.
    7. Sometimes a woman wants nothing more than for you to share her emotions with her. A woman stands there like a tuning fork vibrating at a certain frequency; she wants you to pick up her frequency and start vibrating with her.

8. A poor family shepherd can easily ruin a family. If a family shepherd is off balance, the whole family wobbles. A fish rots from the head down.

9. Men are not as sensitive to personal feelings as women. When it comes to feelings, women are like butterflies; men are like buffaloes.

10. Just because you go to church doesn't make you a Christian. Just because you sit in a garage doesn't make you a car.

Here are some great word pictures found in Proverbs.

1. Like vinegar to the teeth and smoke to the eyes, so is the lazy one to those who send him (Prov. 10:26).

2. As a ring of gold in a swine's snout, so is a beautiful woman who lacks discretion (Prov. 11:22).

3. Like apples of gold in settings of silver is a word spoken in right circumstances (Prov. 25:11).

4. Like clouds and wind without rain is a man who boasts of his gifts falsely (Prov. 25:14).

5. Like a bad tooth and an unsteady foot is confidence in a faithless man in time of trouble (Prov. 25:19).

6. Like a trampled spring and a polluted well is a righteous man who gives way before the wicked (Prov. 25:26).

7. Like a city that is broken into and without walls is the man who has no control over his spirit (Prov. 25:28).

8. Like a dog that returns to its vomit is a fool who repeats his folly (Prov. 26:11).

9. Like charcoal to hot embers and wood to fire, so is a contentious man to kindle strife (Prov. 26:21).

10. A constant dripping on a day of steady rain and a contentious woman are alike (Prov. 27:15).

11. Iron sharpens iron, so one man sharpens another (Prov. 27:17).

Appendix F

Dad the Family Shepherd
Prayer Guide

Ephesians 6:4, 12, 18: And, fathers, do not provoke your children to anger, but bring them up in the discipline and instruction of the Lord. . . . For our struggle is not against flesh and blood, but against the rulers, against the powers, against the world forces of this darkness, against the spiritual forces of wickedness in the heavenly places. . . . With all prayer and petition pray at all times in the Spirit, and with this in view, be on the alert with all perseverance and petition for all the saints.

INSTRUCTIONS

1. Form an E-Team (Encouragement Team) by challenging a few other fathers to meet with you once a week for four weeks to pray for your children. You should have at least five men but not more than seven on your E-Team.

2. Choose a convenient and private place to meet. We suggest meeting at 6:45 A.M. so you can meet for an hour and not be late for work.

3. During each meeting, follow the format suggested below. In addition to praying for your family, please pray for Dave Simmons and Dad the Family Shepherd.

EXPLANATION

1. These four family shepherd prayer guides are based on Luke 2:52:

And Jesus kept increasing in wisdom and stature, and in favor with God and men.

Meeting 1: Focus on your child's wisdom.
Meeting 2: Focus on your child's stature.
Meeting 3: Focus on your child's spiritual life.
Meeting 4: Focus on your child's social life.

Appendix F

2. Each meeting should have these 4 parts:
   5 min: Each man give a brief report on his family.
   5 min: Read the verses in the guide.
   40 min: Pray for the children.
   10 min: Pray for each other and your wives.

Meeting 1: Pray for wisdom for your child.
1. Take no more than five minutes to give family reports.
2. Read these verses: Prov. 2:1-6; 3:13-18; 4:20-22
3. Pray for your children:
   - That they will acquire wisdom and discernment and make practical use of it.
   - That they will gain understanding and common sense.
   - That they will make wisdom a central part of their lives.
   - That you fathers will carry out your responsibility to transfer wisdom to your children.

Meeting 2: Pray for your child's stature.
1. Take no more than five minutes to give family reports.
2. Read these verses:
      Prov. 4:20-23; 3:21-24; Matt. 6:25-34
3. Pray for your children:
   - That they will enjoy a healthy, sound body.
   - That they will enjoy good rest and sleep.
   - That they will trust God for all of their bodily needs.
   - That you fathers will be good models in trusting God for your needs.

Meeting 3: Pray for your child's spiritual life.
1. Take no more than five minutes to give family reports.
2. Read these verses:
      2 Tim. 3:14-17; Ps. 97:10; John 17:15; James 4:7
3. Pray for your children:
   - That they will trust Christ at any early age.
   - That they will have a hatred for sin.
   - That they will be protected from the evil one.
   - That they will submit to God and actively resist Satan in all circumstances.
   - That you fathers will disciple your children.

Meeting 4: Pray for your child's social life.
1. Take no more than five minutes to give family reports.
2. Read these verses:
      Dan. 6:3; Prov. 1:10-11; Hosea 2:6; Rom. 13:1
3. Pray for your children:
   - That they will have an extraordinary attitude of responsibility.
   - That they will desire the right kind of friends and be protected from the wrong kind of friends.
   - That they will be hedged in so they cannot find their way to wrong people or wrong places and that the wrong people cannot find their way to them.
   - That they will be kept from the wrong mate and saved for the right one.
   - That they will respect those in authority over them.
   - That you fathers will be great friends with your children and model friendship for them.

Appendix G

The Ten Phases of Childhood Development

1. The Unborn Phase (-9 mos.–birth).
Unborn babies can think, feel, and control their bodies. They respond to mother and to stimuli from outside the womb. They are immature in every area of life except one: they are eternal spirits, fully human and written in God's Book of Life (see Ps. 139:13-16).

2. The Creeper Phase (birth–12 mos.).
The child is extremely dependent and needs lots of attention, physical cuddling, and sensory stimulation. The love and affection the child gets helps form a basic worldview and attitude toward life. The child begins sex affiliation and a basic self-concept. The pain pool begins to fill and the child faces the fork in the road that leads either to a shame-based or honor-based personality. The child must master ways to overcome rejection. The child needs plenty of sleep.

3. The Toddler Phase (12 mos.–24 mos.).
Endowed with boundless energy, the hyperactive child enters the age of inquisitive exploration—read "getting into trouble." The house must be child-proofed. The child begins walking, talking, and starts potty training—wanting lots of verbal interaction and word games. The child notices sex differences, learns names for different parts, and the sex differentiation of the father begins to have an effect. The child needs freedom to explore but can start learning boundaries.

4. The Dynamo Phase (24 mos.–36 mos.).
The baby faces its first major crisis: breaking up the baby identity and reconstructing an infant/child persona. This turbulent task makes the child negative, defiant, and abrasive. The child attacks the problem of ego-strength and needs boundaries but lots of flexibility and understanding. His toilet training should be finished and boys begin to copy dad while girls begin to adapt to him. Be careful of too much strict control and using force to achieve conformity. Remember, this too shall pass.

5. The Social Phase (3–5).
Muscular and motor skills expand at a rapid rate and the child needs greater range and space. The child begins to drift away from parent exclusivity and wants to make friends. The child needs to increase risk-taking and begins to express emotions. The child begins to ask questions and investigate sexual matters, and becomes conscious of the body development and performance. The child establishes sexual preference with a close relationship and modeling with the parent of the same sex. The child begins to understand the concepts of work, performance, and competition, and can grasp religious ideas is a concrete way.

6. The Buddy Phase (6–8).
The child now becomes a playaholic and gets serious about the business of having fun. The child likes noisy, violent, active high-energy activities and doesn't know when to slow down. The child dives into intensive relationships with peers, establishes intimate bonding with playmates, and loves sports, field games, and parlor games. Gender role identity causes children to attach closely with the parent of the opposite sex. The child becomes very peer conscious and wants to go along with the crowd in fear of being left out. This is the phase where friendship principles are learned, so extended times with friends should be allowed, along with group activities, spend-the-night parties, and trips. The child reaches the important phase where conceptual and abstract thinking can be done. Present behavior can be associated with future consequences, and the child can begin to subordinate present wishes for future gains.

7. The Modeler Phase (9–11).
The child plateaus here and bunches up for the great spring into puberty just ahead. The child consolidates the progress to date and concentrates on stability, security, and consistency. Ethical, moral, and value systems are solidified. Boys and girls display great dislike for each other which is merely the lull before the storm. Children develop great loyalty to friends of the same sex and develop concentrated attachment to the parent of the same sex. They polish up gender role identity. Girls move ahead in verbal and emotional areas of life.

8. The Puberty Phase (12–14).
Everything breaks loose. Put them in a barrel and feed them through the cork-hole. They start leaking, swelling, and smelling. Strange hormones gush through and push out hair and acne in all the awkward places and they obsess on sex. They gorge on food, the badder the better. The body dominates and self becomes the center of the sun's orbit. They tend to break down the childhood persona and form a young adult identity much the same way they did in the Dynamo stage. In fact, puberty is the terrible twos in wide vision technicolor. They begin to break away from parents. Parents need to start relating more as counselor/encourager rather than trainer. Encourage group activities and forbid pairing off because of mature temptation and childlike inner controls. They are quite capable of maintaining a spiritual walk with the Lord through this time. The church youth department becomes crucial because so much depends on the condition of their peers.

9. The Adolescence Phase (15–17)
Full physical maturity is achieved. The boys begin to catch up with the girls. They begin to zero in on special abilities, skills, and talents. Life after family occupies their minds as they break away and start their own path through life. The youth culture becomes a great enemy of Christian life. Boys become extremely preoccu-

pied with sex and adopt phallic symbols and rituals while experimenting with gender role on girls. Girls desire emotional intimacy with boys and can easily mistake sex for the male fellowship they need. This is the time that tries men's souls. Whatever the cost, try to keep communication open.

10. The Quest Phase (18–24).

This is the age of dreams and teamwork. Now, more than ever, the individual moves into intense relationships that require interpersonal skills. They encounter college roommates, marriage, and start their career, all of which require the development of a sophisticated level of interdependence. They must fracture the youth identity they painstakingly built up and put themselves back together as an adult. They experience great anxiety as they look outward and forward to the future. This can be one of the most difficult times in the parent/child relationship. They need as much support from parents at this time as ever but also need to be allowed to drift out of the family. A rite of passage and a paternal blessing for life is essential at this time.

Appendix H

The Four Gauges
of Maturity

THE MENTAL GAUGE

What a change thirteen years can make: a baby thinks that you cease to exist if you get beyond his vision and hearing, while a teenager thinks he ceases to exist if he is not seen and heard. This points out the obvious fact that children undergo an incredible degree of change in their thinking abilities as they grow up. What's not so obvious is that parents fail to take this into consideration in the Equipping process.

Mental accomplishment is a prerequisite for moral and cooperation development. The latter two can proceed only as rapidly as the mental development occurs.

The maturity of a child's thinking ability determines what you teach the child, how you train the child, and what discipline methodology you employ. After reviewing extensive research on this topic, I have simplified and condensed the material on the evolution of thinking into the following three levels.

The Concrete Thinking Stage

This stage features sensorimotor thinking which is simple, basic reaction thinking. The infant has no concept of self and does not know of the existence of other people and things unless they are intruding and stimulating one of the five senses. The infant can only entertain one idea at a time and cannot relate effect with cause.

The Logical Thinking Stage

The mind begins to figure out logical ways to relate to people, things, and other parts of the environment. The mind can begin to identify, classify, analyze, and file thoughts. Cause and effect are now possible and consequences can be associated with behaviors. Emotions can be identified and expressed in primitive ways. Multiple ideas can be processed. Ideas can be connected in chains. Actions and behaviors can be planned to lead to desired consequences. Imagination operates impulsively with little control.

The Conceptual Thinking Stage

The mind attains the capacity to "go outside itself" and see the person in context with the environment. Abstract concepts can be processed and acted on. Values and principles can be analyzed and internalized. The mind can establish convictions with which to screen and select behaviors. Imagination can be controlled and channeled into complex problem-solving. The ability to empathize and develop a keen awareness of others and their uniqueness is possible.

THE MORAL GAUGE

Can you imagine a father grabbing a one-year-old boy and yelling at him, "Son, when are you going to start treating others like you want to be treated?" Instead of the boy observing the Golden Rule, he would end up modifying it to state, "I'd better hurt others before they hurt me."

We all too often expect elementary school children to operate on an advanced morality system far beyond their capability. A family shepherd must understand that the development of morality is a long-range process and must be built experience upon experience, and precept upon precept, until the child reaches the third stage where his or her life is founded on principles and convictions.

The Self-Focus Stage

This initial stage follows closely the concrete thinking stage. The limited thinking capacity reduces the idea of right and wrong to the simple standard of: It is good if it makes me feel good; it is bad if it hurts me. Morality is based entirely on immediate impact on the senses. The instinct of survival and growth determines ethics and values.

Examples:

1. It would be right to beat up my friend and take his toy because it would be fun to play with it.

2. It would be right to steal the baby's food because I am hungry.

The Others'-Focus Stage

Outside controls characterize this stage of morality development. At first, what is good or bad depends on how it impacts others. If it pleases them, it is good; if it displeases them, it is bad. This advanced moral development is crucial because it takes the child out of self-centeredness, but it causes serious problems as well. The child can end up adopting the sense of moral values, good or bad, held by the significant others that surround him or her.

As this stage progresses, a child begins to categorize the opinions of others and formulate a doctrinal code of rules, regulations, and procedures. This law of standards becomes the child's sense of right and wrong. The danger again is that this forms a foundation for situational ethics and value clarification (read "value reduction"). The codex shifts and changes to comply with the general sources of input. This leads to a life of unpredictability and creates havoc in the community.

Examples:

1. It is right for communist children in China to turn in their parents for political crimes against the state.

2. It is right to take money from one person, keep some, and give the rest to others (lunch money theft at school or income redistribution in the U.S.A.).

3. It is right to have premarital sex because adults promote it and all the other kids are doing it.

4. It is right to cheat in school (income tax), because everyone else does and if I don't, my grades (refund) will suffer.

The Principle-Focus Stage
Ethics and morality rise above the temporary opinions of those around me. Moral judgment is based on the proven principles that have successfully governed community life over a long period of time. These findings are consolidated into ethical principles that become convictions that can override instinctive impulses and situational factors. At this stage, a person subordinates everything to these inner convictions.

Examples:

1. I have a conviction against cheating so I will not copy someone else's homework.

2. I have a conviction against taxation without representation so I will cry out, "Give me liberty or give me death."

3. I have a conviction about committing fornication so I will not engage in premarital sex.

THE BEHAVIOR GAUGE
Babies are out of control, and if you get one, you'll soon notice their ability to get everything else out of control. But, as children mature, so does their ability to control their behavior. At first, behavior is instinctive and random. Later on, children begin to learn the rules and play the game to achieve their best advantage. Finally, they learn to subordinate their behavior to a set of inner principles.

The Instinctive Stage
When children are first born, all behavior is instinctive. They seek food, companionship, hygiene, and protection out of instinct. During this stage, you obviously don't try to exercise control over the child. Rewards and discipline are ineffective. The child simply cannot distinguish between right and wrong or cause and effect.

The Modification Stage
Now, small children can begin to associate specific behavior with immediate consequences. Immediate is the key.

They soon pass from instinctive behavior to a stage where their behavior can be modified by external factors. Here, babies begin to learn which specific behaviors bring rewards and which ones remain fruitless. During this phase the parents can practice behavior modification with some degree of success if they realize the following:

1. The consequences must be immediate and short. The life span of conscious guilt in small children is about ten seconds, so if you don't correct them within that small window, they can't make the association between your discipline and their behavior. They think you are just being mean to them.

2. This is a difficult but necessary transition phase and definitely not effective in the long run.

3. Even as you enter this phase, you should be eagerly working toward getting out of it into the next phase.

4. Spanking (as a corrective measure and never for punishment—see chap. 8) should be limited to this phase only. I do not recommend spanking in the instinctive or perception phase.

The Perception Stage
The goal is to get children into the perception phase of behavior control as soon as possible. This can start anywhere from six to eight. Here, the children's minds have

developed to the point where their perceptions of life begin to govern their behavior. Here they begin conceptual and abstract thinking. They finally gain the capacity to make the connection between values, behavior, and desired results.

Now children can begin to exercise intrinsic control over their behavior. They have reached that stage where their perceptions influence behavior. They begin to experiment with the effects of subordinating their behavior to their value system. This is the time you hope that God's "heart-ware" kicks in.

THE COOPERATION GAUGE

Another primary test of maturity is the level of ability to cooperate with others. Man is not an island: Man is an archipelago. Life must be lived in community, not in isolation. Immature people cannot subordinate self to the good of the community. Mature people know how to cooperate and capture the synergism that comes with community teamwork.

In the continuum from birth to maturity, a child must pass through three degrees of social integration: total dependence, independence, and interdependence.

I always thought my goal for Helen and Brandon was to get them to a maturity stage characterized by complete independence. But, now I know better. Independence is a necessary transition phase but a damaging phase in which to bog down. My goal is to get them out of dependence (zero cooperation), through independence, and on to a level called interdependence — sophisticated cooperation and teamwork.

Total Dependence
Babies start out utterly dependent — in total reliance on others for survival. They progress naturally through the phases of childhood development until they gain the ability to break the shackles of their dependency by coping with life on their own.

Careful Independence
Children soon phase into a stage where they gain moderate self-control and begin to "own" themselves. This autonomy is essential, but problems arise when a child gets locked into it and stays focused on self. Me-ism takes over and the youth gets cut off from intimacy and teamwork with others. Independence was meant to be a transition stage for the gathering and control of self so that it could be managed in cooperation with others in the next stage — interdependence.

Healthy Interdependence
A person in this stage possesses all the strengths of the independent phase (like self-reliance and capability to cope) but has a strong character, is in control, and chooses to cooperate with others in a mutually enhancing community. It's in this final stage where people can run on godly "heart-ware," subordinate selfish instincts, choose to cooperate with others (the group, team, family, etc.) in mutual enhancement, and enjoy the synergism and deep gratification of relationships and teamwork.